The Real Estate Market

SUCKS

Now What?

8 Ways to Save or Sell Your Home

KEN BEASLEY

New York

The Real Estate Market Sucks, Now What?
8 Ways to Save or Sell Your Home

Cover Design by: 3 Dog Design: www.3dogdesign.net

ISBN 978-1-60037-613-9

Library of Congress Control Number: 2009924309

MORGAN · JAMES
THE ENTREPRENEURIAL PUBLISHER

Morgan James Publishing, LLC
1225 Franklin Ave., STE 325
Garden City, NY 11530-1693
Toll Free 800-485-4943
www.MorganJamesPublishing.com

In an effort to support local communities, raise awareness and funds, Morgan James Publishing donates one percent of all book sales for the life of each book to Habitat for Humanity. Get involved today, visit **www.HelpHabitatForHumanity.org**.

PREFACE
Profiting in Today's Real Estate Market

The Equity Share Group has been providing "creative approaches" to buying and selling real estate in both California and Nevada since 1984. As early as the mid-1980's, we recognized the need to create alternative ways to get into the housing market and build our version of the "AMERICAN DREAM."

With the current state of the real estate market, the Equity Share Group approach to "creative real estate" will apply to a broader segment of the market. Buyers trying to relocate from areas that are depressed, divorced buyers, move-up buyers, and buyers who have been hurt because of the decline. All need a "creative approach."

This book will answer questions about the benefits of "HOME OWNERSHIP," and is directed to buyers, investors, and private lenders, to help them protect their investments over the next few years.

To be "creative" in real estate you must understand the process of buying and selling, be sure you are well educated in all aspects, choose a knowledgeable professional to work with, and finally never get into a transaction that will cause you to end up in a worse situation than before you started. Never buy, sell, or invest with your emotions.

Two of the most important words I want you to understand before you get into the real estate market are "PATIENCE" and "REALITY." Look at the purchase of a property as an investment. How long will you hold the property, what improvements will you need, and always what is your exit plan?

In closing, understanding real estate, and developing a comfort level with the process, will be one of the most rewarding and self-fulfilling goals you can achieve in your life.

Table of Contents

Preface. iii

Acknowledgments. vii

Introduction ix

CHAPTERS

1   The Real Estate Perfect Storm 1

2   Renting Versus Ownership 5

3   Buying and Selling Real Estate – the Creative Approach 11

4   The Ups and Downs of the Real Estate Market 25

5   The Concept of Equity Sharing/Joint Ownership 29

6   The Lease Option Conversion Program. 61

7   The Concept of Contract of Sale. .75

8   Lowering Your Mortgage Payment—"Loan Modification" . . .93

9   The Concept of the Short Sale. 97

10   Foreclosure 109

11   Bankruptcy. 131

12   REOs (Real Estate/Bank Owned Properties). 143

13   The 1031 Exchange. 149

14   The Pros and Cons of "Creative Real Estate". 169

15   Conclusion 175

TERMS AND DEFINITIONS 177

ACKNOWLEDGMENTS

Gaining the knowledge necessary to be versed in all aspects of real estate requires many years of exploring different approaches to buying and selling real estate. Think outside the box and you will be able to survive both the good and the bad times.

As a real estate broker in both California and Nevada it became apparent to me that the only way I could compete with larger real estate companies was to offer something different.

In 1975, I was fortunate to be able to open my own title and escrow company. My wife, BJ, and I started with one office in Carson City, Nevada. In two years our company grew to thirty employees and four locations. Your "AMERICAN DREAM" can come true if you only take the chance.

Don't let someone tell you that you can't buy a home. Many real estate professionals only want clients who have a 10% to 20% down payment and perfect credit. I always felt that, in order to be a good real estate professional, I should look for ways to help people reach their goals. I am writing this book to show the consumer that, whether you are buying or selling, you do have alternatives. If, by reading the information presented here, you are able to learn a little about the "creative" approaches of equity sharing, contracts of sale, short sales, lease options, and foreclosures, then I have achieved my goal.

The purpose of this book is to also educate the average buyer, seller, investor, and real estate agent on different subjects. I have had a diversified background in title, exchanging, commercial, and general real estate. Much of my knowledge came from taking some risks, but mostly from taking courses offered by the real estate boards across the country. Several CPAs and attorneys have been also been nice enough to educate me on the things that can and can't be done when dealing with real estate.

Since 1971, I have been fortunate enough to be guided by special people in my life. My wife's and my family helped us get started in our first business. Without BJ's encouragement and support I would never have had the confidence to start my first business, and I would not be the person I am today. I've been married for 36 years, and I'm very lucky to not only have a great partner, but to also have her as my best friend.

I would also like to thank my Equity Share Group staff; especially Diane Mietzel, Barbara Jensen and Donna Kaufman for helping me edit this book, with an additional thank you to Barbara Jensen for the design, layout, and production.

INTRODUCTION

The biggest investment in any person's life is "home ownership." The selling and buying of real estate is the process of accomplishing your goal of wealth building and personal achievement.

The first-time home buyer needs guidance to accomplish his/her goal of building equity in their property. The investor needs to look at the purchase of real estate with the idea of how to hold onto it, and expand his/her wealth. The question and answer sections will look at the following subjects:

This book creates a space for

- understanding the real estate market
- the importance of "home ownership"
- the ups and downs of the real estate market
- learning about the "creative concepts" of equity sharing
- contract of sale
- lease option
- short sale, and
- the structure of foreclosures and bankruptcies.

The buying and selling of real estate comes with many benefits, the primary goal being, besides a place to live, is equity build-up and tax write-offs.

We all know there are conventional ways to buy real estate. If you have a down payment and excellent credit, "home ownership" will be right around the corner for you. But, what happens to the buyer or seller who needs a "creative approach" in order to be able to deal in the real estate market? What alternative way can they seek to achieve "home ownership?" In the chapters to follow, we will examine the alternative ways that are not talked about by conventional real estate agents. The average professional will care about his/her client, but the commission they are going to earn is usually their number one priority. I want you to understand all of the "creative approaches" that will help you to get into a home.

It's not too late to invest in real estate. The current real estate market is good for buying, and the longer you wait, the harder it will be to accomplish your goals. If you are able to learn from the different approaches presented here, you will some day thank me for introducing you to "the future of real estate."

"THE REAL ESTATE PERFECT STORM"

CHAPTER ONE

"THE REAL ESTATE PERFECT STORM"

The reason I started the book with this chapter is obvious. Given the state of the economy, it was apparent to me that someone needed to explain to people what is happening with the real estate market. I know so many people who are trying to survive the current market, hoping that they can save the assets they have and be able to invest in the future.

The "real estate perfect storm" relates to how, when everything goes wrong, the consequences can create a huge problem. When lenders are making sub-prime loans, property values are declining by 40%, and the market cannot support the current inventory, the real estate perfect storm is created.

Consumers have nowhere to go; their job status is under attack; they can't sell or refinance their home; and the home next door is renting for $1,500 less than their mortgage payment. The stock market is down; major companies are going under; and the government is trying to put a Band-Aid on any problem that comes up. The trend is to try to stop the dam from bursting, but the real game plan is to find a solution without causing a major flood. Can it be done? I don't think so, under the current atmosphere, but I do think that we can address alternative methods to try to solve the existing problems. Today's real estate market and the financial markets are in shambles, and all sectors of society are feeling the effects of the sub-prime loan crisis.

How did this all happen? It happened because of the surging real estate market from 2001 through 2006. The aggressive loan programs put out by lenders and the loose credit standards, combined with risky adjustable loans, all contributed to the current crisis. What is happening now actually started in 2004, when lenders were approving loans with nothing down and no verification of income—and using inflated appraisals. If only we had understood that the bubble was about to burst, it would have been possible to have addressed the problem before it all came crashing down. The two main factors that contributed to the beginning of the real estate perfect storm were the financial market crisis and the extreme downturn of the housing market.

The sub-prime mortgage crisis began with the downfall of the United States housing bubble and the high delinquency rate in adjustable rate mortgages. Prior to 2005 and 2006, most lenders and borrowers depended on the rising housing values to correct any deficiencies in the real estate market. Most borrowers were able to refinance their loans and pay off existing loans to give them more time. Unfortunately, once interest rates started to rise and housing values declined, refinancing became more difficult, and the number of loan defaults began to go up dramatically, as interest rates re-adjusted.

As home prices went down and homeowners fell behind on their payments, their mortgage amounts grew to more than the value of the property. The real estate perfect storm was starting to move forward with a vengeance! In 2006, foreclosures started to increase nationally. This acceleration, along with the lack of cooperation from lenders, triggered the financial crisis.

By the beginning of 2007, the number of foreclosures was up a staggering 79% nationally, with no solution in sight. Banks and mortgage companies examined the possibility of short sales and re-writing loans, but, with very little cooperation and no real game plan, the major lending institutions started to report huge losses. This led to a national credit crunch that affected world markets, which in turn, affected Wall Street.

As lenders and banks failed, the economy and the stock market showed the effects. Case in point, on September 29, 2008, $1 trillion was lost. Did you know that by the end of 2008, over 2 million foreclosures took place in the United States? Lenders are really the ones who caused this rise in the number of delinquencies. In the old days, banks created loans and kept them in their portfolios. The new approach has been for lenders to sell their loans to investors. Today's financial institutions are going under, and most lenders are saddled with billions of dollars in bad loans. No investor is going to purchase bad debt.

Banks around the world, concerned with the United States market, tried to infuse funds into the system with the hope of restoring liquidity in the commercial paper market. The knee-jerk reaction to the problem resulted in the final straw that hit the stock market on September 29, 2008. The Federal Reserve panicked and cut interest rates, and Congress did a bailout in February of 2008—all designed to stimulate the economy. The funny, and sad, thing about all of this is that the investors on Wall Street who made their money buying "discounted notes" did not believe in the methods used to stimulate the economy.

The lenders and investors on Wall Street and the government have caused the downfall of the economy. The projected bailout will cost approximately $700 billion, and neither Wall Street nor the economy will ever be the same.

Let's take all of this information and bring it down to why a couple I will call "Mr. and Mrs. Smith" are losing their home. In 2005, like millions of other Americans, the Smiths went to a lender to get a loan to purchase a home. They had found the home of their dreams; their credit reports were done; and they had the minimum down payment money, so the Smiths were able to purchase a beautiful three-bedroom, two-bathroom home in a great area.

The first deed of trust on the property was for $475,000, and the mortgage payment had the adjustable option that gave them payment choices — minimum payment, interest only, and principle/interest. And, with home ownership came other obligations, such as insurance, property taxes, and home owners association (HOA) fees. The Smiths opted to pay the minimum mortgage payment of $2,100 a month, to be able to comfortably afford their other obligations. Since the economy was growing at a minimum of 10% a year, the Smiths hoped that the growth would take care of the over $600 a month negative—adding up to about $7,200 a year.

However, in 2006, the economy started to decline, and as the Smiths' mortgage payment increased, the job market also got worse. The real estate perfect storm was now hitting home for the Smiths. The payment of less than interest only and the loan payment adjusting up, along with falling home prices and lenders clamping down on credit, were seriously affecting the Smiths, like millions of other people.

In 2007, the Smiths' home declined over 20% in value, making the home worth only $400,000, and their loan increased from $475,000 to $489,000, because of the negative add-on. The Smiths were in trouble—they couldn't sell their property, and they couldn't refinance; all they could do was watch their dream of home ownership and financial security slip away.

The Smiths could have rented a home like theirs in the same neighborhood for $2,000 a month. Instead, they were paying over $3,300 a month, trying to save their home, but only losing equity.

How can the Smiths get out from under their obligation? If it comes down to missing payments and being foreclosed on, they can look into either doing a short sale or filing for bankruptcy, but, unfortunately, both of these exit plans will ruin their credit, cause duress, and create a no-win situation for all parties.

Mr. and Mrs. Smith now wish they had taken more time to analyze their purchase in 2005. If they would have bought a less expensive home, put more money down, gotten a fixed rate loan, and been realistic with their lender about what they earned and what they could really afford their situation could have been minimized.

Unfortunately, in 2008, the Smiths lost their home to foreclosure, and sadly, their plight has been duplicated over and over again throughout the country. The bailout recovery plan might work, but none of us will know the effects until the real estate market has hit bottom.

When demand exceeds supply, and consumers feel confident that they can get a good buy on a home, with a good loan, then maybe the economy will have some hope of recovery. And, when the government and investors are willing to contribute or extend new capital to financial institutions to make decent loans, we might see a light at the end of the tunnel.

In the upcoming chapters, we'll discuss some alternative ways to buy, sell, and profit in today's real estate market. The "future of real estate" needs help!

CHAPTER TWO

RENTING VERSUS OWNERSHIP

The current market conditions are very unusual, so when comparing whether to rent versus owning a home, you must analyze your own individual needs. On the bright side, if you do choose to own a home, property values in most parts of the country have declined from 30% to 50% over the past year so there are some great buys out there.

If you have recently lost a home, or haven't decided if now is the right time to get into the real estate market, then this chapter will offer some insights into the benefits of renting versus the benefits of ownership, and how they will affect you in the long run.

As the housing market declines and more properties are foreclosed on investors will buy up the distressed inventory, making more rentals available to the open market.

When that happens, rents will go up throughout the country. People need to be educated as to the benefits of ownership versus renting.

Only 30% of the people in California can afford to own a home. It's usually easier to pay someone a monthly rent than to worry about the problems that can come with owning property. In reality, most people would love to own the home they occupy, but never really set goals for themselves. I'm here to tell you—"home ownership" is possible!"

This chapter is going to cover seven reasons why it's better to own than rent.

The questions you should ask yourself about "RENTING versus OWNERSHIP," are as follows:

a. **Which choice offers more value?**
Paying rent results in one thing, the value of getting that receipt for paying your monthly obligation. Sure, you have a place to live, but remember, it's not your home, you can't make alterations, you usually can't have a pet, and, in reality, you must abide by the rules of the "LANDLORD."

When you own a home, your monthly mortgage is not wasted. It accrues equity for you. A loan payment is made up of principal, interest, taxes and insurance. The "principal" reduction results in equity build-up, and is like a forced savings account. Your "interest" part of the payment is an IRS tax write-off. The property tax proration (monthly portion) is a tax write-off, so it's apparent that rental payments are not as beneficial as mortgage payments. With new loan programs, most home buyers realize that mortgage payments, and rents, are almost equal in most states.

b. **Which method offers more stability?**
One of the negative aspects of your monthly rental payments is that you are usually at the mercy of your landlord. Your rental payments increase each year, and, the only one that benefits from these increases is the property owner/landlord.

When a person buys a property, they normally take out a loan against the property. The lender, for loaning the money, receives a document called a "deed of trust/note" against the home (property). This document states that the buyer/borrower owes the lender the balance of the money. This money will be paid back, in monthly installments, and will be paid off over an estimated thirty years, depending on the structure of the loan. The lender will set the payments at a fixed monthly amount that will be affordable to the buyer, (buyer must qualify for the loan). The buyer, unlike the renter, will have a monthly payment that will usually be fixed, and remain stable for the duration of the loan. The renter will probably have an increase in his/her monthly obligation each year, without any additional benefits.

c. **Which method offers tax benefits?**
    The renter has no tax benefits, and, other than the convenience of being able to move at a moment's notice, there will never be a benefit to the person who does not own his/her home. The property owner can almost count on saving enough in tax benefits to be able to afford any increase in expenses that "home ownership" might bring. At the end of the tax year, the mortgage interest for a property owner will be deducted from the income earned during that tax year. (e.g., if you made $80,000 in that tax year, and the mortgage interest you paid for the year, plus property taxes, added up to $22,000, then your taxable income for the year would be $58,000, rather than the original $80,000.)

    The owner would also have the right to deduct related tax expenses, depending on the status of the property. If you are employed, not self-employed, you must have an agreement with your employer to have taxes withheld from your paycheck. The average person declares deductions, either 0, 1, 2 or more, depending on whether or not they have children, own property, or have the capability, at the end of the year, to come up with the extra money needed to pay the IRS. When you own your home, and have interest write-offs, you can usually raise your deductions from the low of 0 to a maximum of 7. This tax advantage can give you an estimated $350 or more, every month on your paycheck, without any further tax liability. Tax write-offs allow you to keep more of your own money rather than giving it to the IRS.

d. **Which method gives you greater strength in building good credit?**
    A renter's stability is always questioned when dealing with a bank, retail store, or any credit-type industry. It's not that you are not trustworthy, but the stability is often not there, especially if you have moved a number of times over recent years. "Home ownership" is recognized as a major indicator of financial integrity, stability and commitment. Many lenders will give you equity loans, based on the equity in your property. Lenders want to secure their loans based on

"real property." Employers sometimes take into account the stability of "home ownership" when considering an application. Assets and value play a large part in being able to secure a loan to buy an automobile, furniture, or an expensive personal item.

e. **Which choice helps you establish roots?**

When you rent, you are more mobile, and often do not establish roots in a given location. Earlier, I mentioned that one of the advantages of renting is that you can move from place-to-place much easier than when you own property. Be careful! Make sure that you understand the concept of renting because a contract to be a tenant is legal and binding, and you must abide by the terms of the agreement. If you violate the rental agreement the landlord can keep your deposit, take you to court, or seek damages for the destruction to his/her property. As a renter, you are also at the mercy of your previous landlord when it comes to giving you a good reference for future rental consideration. "Home ownership" will give you and your family security, pride, and, most importantly, community involvement. Your family will feel that they belong, and have protection from being controlled by outside influences. "Home ownership" allows a family to be a part of the school district, churches and communities in a way that builds character and lasting relationships.

f. **Does owning a home provide more living space?**

When you rent an apartment you are usually limited to a basic floor plan, limited storage space, and you seldom have a covered garage. Renting is more for convenience rather than permanent stability. Most apartments aren't three and four bedrooms, and forget about having a pet— since most rentals don't have a yard. Renting a home might give you more room and allow for pets but, the areas, schools, and the style of homes you have to choose from are often limited.

When you purchase a home, it's in the area you where want to live. "Home ownership" allows you to pick the schools you want your children to attend and the community you want to be a part of. "Home ownership" allows you to choose the style of home you want to live in, the type of landscaping that will enhance your property value, the colors you want to use to decorate your home, and even the fixtures that you want to enjoy on a daily basis. In my many years in real estate, I have never found anyone who really enjoyed renting versus the benefits of owning his/her own property.

g. Is owning a home a good investment opportunity?

Investment opportunities are important in our lives, and can take on many forms—investment in stocks, investment in personal items, investment in savings accounts, and, the greatest potential for wealth, the investment in real estate. The investment in real estate takes two forms:

1. **Home ownership** – The investment in real estate, that is your permanent residence, is very important for a number of reasons. First, you get to live in your investment, while it's working for you. The tax benefits alone make it worth the effort to try to achieve "home ownership". Building wealth, in the investment of a home to live in, comes in the following ways — interest deduction, equity build-up, mortgage reduction, and finally appreciation in the overall economy in which you reside. Since 1997, the IRS has had a system in place that states, if you have a permanent residence, you will not be taxed on profit of sale, if you hold onto the property for two years. There would be a $500,000 profit exemption in the sale of your home. For most people this will exempt them from paying taxes to the IRS, on the sale of the home where they live. No taxes means more money in your pocket from "Home ownership." These exemptions allow the husband $250,000, the wife, $250,000, and unmarried individuals, $250,000.

2. **Investment Property** – The ownership of an investment property is different than that of a permanent residence. The majority of this country's wealthiest individuals started with investing in real estate. An investor looks at the purchase of real estate in a different way than the purchaser of a permanent residence. First of all, the investor is not living in the property, so emotions are

not involved, and the return on the investment is the bottom line. Income property, (duplex, apartment building, warehouse, or home rental) relies on return on the investment compared with monthly output.

If you rent a home for $1,200 a month, and your mortgage payment is $900, you must still account for the property taxes (pro-rated monthly), insurance, upkeep/maintenance, and property management. It's not easy to make a return on income property, but if you purchase the investment at the right price, and can make improvements, to give you a better return in the long run, it can be profitable. Rental property falls under different IRS regulations (Section 1031) than a permanent residence, so the investor can write-off mortgage interest and property taxes like a permanent residence. Additionally, the investor can deduct the expenses of property management, maintenance, insurance, depreciation, and any other costs incurred in the operation of the property, as an investment. The investor must declare the income he/she generate from renting the property, and offset it with the expenses. Upon sale of the investment property, the seller can do a tax-exempt exchange, avoiding capital gains on the sale. The 1031 Tax Exchange will be discussed a little later. Remember, you can always convert a permanent residence to a rental property, and a rental property to a permanent residence, if the intent is done in the right way.

I hope this section has convinced you that it's better to purchase a property, rather than rent a property. It's easy for me to make that statement, because I love renters. As a property owner/investor, renters are helping me gain wealth. During the course of this book, I will make suggestions that will show you how you can achieve "home ownership." Remember, do not give up, set your goals, and be patient. Statistics show that owning a home gives you a stronger sense of security, privacy, and credibility—and also helps to build a stronger economy.

"GO FOR HOME OWNERSHIP AND YOU WILL WIN!"
The economy will dictate when you should buy or sell real estate.

CHAPTER THREE

BUYING AND SELLING REAL ESTATE — THE CREATIVE APPROACH

For you to fully understand the process of buying and selling real estate, it is important to learn about the current economy. Before a buyer or seller enters into a transaction, he/she must be able to analyze the market and determine if it's a buyers' market, a sellers' market — or no market at all.

Are there loans available to purchase a home? How much do you need to put down? What are the alternative methods available to buy and sell real estate? Is this the right time to buy?

At some point, you will make the decision to either buy or sell, and sometimes it will have to be done out of necessity. If you decide that now is the time, then read this chapter with the thought of preparing yourself for the best results. Always make your decisions based on the market you are dealing with. Never buy with your emotions.

The Process of "Buying and Selling" Real Estate

The process of buying and selling real estate is very important. The average person does not understand the process that needs to take place, nor do they understand what rights they have as a "buyer or seller," in the process. I want you to feel comfortable while reading this section. When you finish, ask yourself, "Am I more prepared now, to direct my realtor to either sell my property, or purchase a property?"

Let's start with the "buyer." This person is usually seeking a goal that has always been out of reach, and is now examining the possibility of accomplishing his/her one desire—"HOME OWNERSHIP."

The current market favors the buyer

QUESTION: As a buyer, what requirements do I address when thinking about "home ownership?"

ANSWER: The first thing to address is where do I want to live? The second is what can I afford? And, finally how can I achieve these goals? Never be discouraged by realtors or related parties who don't share your same desires. Believe me, goals can be reached.

QUESTION: Where should I look for a home, or condo?

ANSWER: The first thing you should think about is where you work, in relationship to where you want to live. Second, address the type of place you would like to live in. Third, look at the possibility of "home ownership" and how it will change your life style. My recommendation is, always look at the worst home in the best neighborhood, rather than the best home in the worst area. Be realistic, and never purchase a property through emotions. Affordability is the main ingredient.

QUESTION: What can I afford as a buyer?

ANSWER: This question is very important and needs to be addressed. First, the one thing you don't want to do is change your life style, to the point where you, cannot afford to accomplish your goal, financially. Secondly, make sure you qualify your needs with a lender and realtor, and get pre-approved for your loan, before moving forward with the purchase of a home.

QUESTION: What does it take to qualify a buyer?

ANSWER: A buyer needs to know how much home he/she can afford to buy, and to analyze carefully how much he/she can afford to pay each month. Finally, the Buyer has to meet with a Lender and be pre-approved, as to the type of loan he/she can get, how much of a loan he/she can afford, what assets he/she has, what type of credit he/she has. Most Lenders will not only analyze the credit worthiness of the Buyer, but will also look at the availability of the cash he/she is using for the down payment. If a buyer is going to purchase Real estate using a "Creative" approach, then different steps will be taken to qualify them for purchase of the property. In later Chapters, you, as the Buyer, can examine the process of "Lease Options" and "Equity Shares." If the Buyer is going to go the "Creative" route, the purchase must still be workable with the Lender and the Seller.

QUESTION: How does a buyer pick a real estate broker?

ANSWER: This is a difficult question. As a professional broker, in both California and Nevada, I want to be fair to my associates. I feel that most buyers need to really analyze the overall picture before choosing a specific realtor. Buyers and sellers have different needs, so the realtor should approach each party's objectives and goals, differently. Buyers need to feel that the real estate agent/broker is willing to work for him/her, even though they might not have enough down payment money, or great credit. If I were trying to purchase a home, I would want the realtor to really listen to my needs, analyze my financial situation, and be realistic about how they can to get me into a home. Personally, I always look for someone who is creative, professional, and willing to be patient.

The current market is harder on the seller

QUESTION: If I am a seller, how can I sell my home?

ANSWER: A seller knows the property they own better than any appraiser, realtor, or other professional. The problem is, most sellers think their property is worth more than it actually is, according to market standards. Just as I advised buyers not to make an emotional purchase, I recommend that all sellers analyze their property and set a realistic value, if they want to expedite the time period of the sale. If the seller can afford to be creative, they will not only get a better asking price, but will open up a market that will make the sale of their home much easier. If you're considering selling your property, make sure that you fix it up so it looks presentable, and never advance large amounts of money to sell your home.

QUESTION: How do I determine a sales price?

ANSWER: You can determine a sales price by the following methods:

    a.   Research comparable sales of properties that are similar to yours in your area. Comparables are only good if the properties that you are comparing have sold in the past six months.

    b.   Have a reputable realtor come out and give you a market analysis on your property, showing you what properties are going for in the area, and what you should list your home for, if it were to be put on the market. Always list your home to be competitive, but do not over price your property. Never attach a dollar amount to emotional value, and always give yourself some room for negotiation.

    c.   Get a formal appraisal.

QUESTION: How does the seller pick a real estate broker to list his/her home?

ANSWER: The unfortunate way is a friend's recommendation of someone they know to represent you. I always feel it's better to do the homework, to determine which professional you should use to make your investment profitable. Most realtors understand that you need to set a price on your home. They should then analyze how much you need to get out of the property to accomplish your goals, and finally, what are you trying to accomplish by selling your property. The professional realtor will do a market analysis, set a price that will sell, and counsel you as to what you want to purchase with your proceeds. There are time restrictions that are important, such as: how long do you have to sell your home? Never let a Realtor talk you into a six-month listing — I always recommend a three month listing, with a month-to-month extension.

QUESTION: What does a seller need to disclose about his/her property before they sell it?

ANSWER: Under most state laws, and real estate laws, sellers are usually required to disclose all defects the property has, at the time they list the property to sell. Realtors have a "disclosure statement" that will need to be completed. This form, signed under oath, states that the seller is disclosing all defects he/she may know about the property, any area problems that might exist with the property and finally, any zoning/boundary problems that might be pre-existing. Any inspections and reports the seller has received on his/her property must be made available to the buyer or his/her real estate agent. Remember that the buyer is encouraged to obtain any inspections deemed necessary to complete the inspection phase of buying and selling a home.

QUESTION: What does the phrase "offer and acceptance" mean?

ANSWER: These are the two essential components of a valid contract, a meeting of the minds. The "offer-or" is the person who makes the offer and the person to whom the offer is made is the "offer-ee." The "offer and acceptance" is sometimes called the "purchase agreement." To make it simple to understand, the "offer and acceptance" is the first stage of a contract, subject to certain terms and conditions. An accepted "offer and acceptance" is a binding contract. "Offer and acceptances" usually have contingencies that spell out the reasons that the buyer or seller could back out of the contract if conditions are not met.

QUESTION: How does a buyer write an offer and acceptance?

ANSWER: Usually the buyer seeks the advice of a real estate broker when writing an "offer and acceptance/purchase agreement." The buyer can write an offer on his/her own, but if you are not represented by an agent, then the seller's agent does not really represent you. The agent might have a fiduciary relationship with you, but your true benefit of negotiation might be hampered. If an agent does represent you, and you have selected the property you want to purchase, then, the first phase is to write the offer. The terms of the offer must reflect the things you want to present to the seller:

 a. Sales Price
 b. Property Description
 c. Terms
 d. Proof of Title Insurance (Preliminary Report)
 e. Disclosure Conditions
 f. Escrow Agent
 g. Loan Information
 h. Home Warranty
 i. Maintenance from Seller of Property
 j. Prorations
 k. Property Taxes and Assessments
 l. Close of Escrow (COE)
 m. Vesting
 n. Conditions of Acceptance
 o. Time Period to Accept the Offer

QUESTION: How does a buyer present the offer and acceptance?

ANSWER: The buyers' agent usually presents the offer to the seller, and either presents the offer personally, or leaves it with the sellers' agent. I do not like this method. I recommend that you always ask to be present at the presentation, and see if it can be presented to the seller personally, and not to his/her agent.

The more the seller knows about you, the buyer, the better the chance your offer will be accepted. As the buyer, never give the seller more than 48-hours to accept your offer. Always have a pre-approved loan letter with the offer, and proof of your willingness to purchase the property. Markets and economies determine if you are in a sellers' market or buyers' market.

My feeling is that when you present an offer for a client, you should always try to find out the motivation of the seller, and try to meet those needs if they make sense. Terms are more important than the sales price. The art of negotiation will determine if you are successful at purchasing your home or if you are going to lose the property to the next buyer. Our "Equity Share Programs" can help you be "creative" when purchasing a property. The conventional process does not work for REOs or short sales.

QUESTION: What does negotiating a contract mean?

ANSWER: Negotiating a contract means a number of different things, but it principally refers to you, the buyer, and the seller, being able to discuss the agreeable, and non-agreeable, terms of the offer. All parties have wants and needs — it's up to the real estate agent (directed by his/her client) to see to the best of his/her capabilities that these needs are accomplished. In negotiating a contract, never think of stealing from the other party. It's better to understand what you want and work on accomplishing that goal. Be prepared, and put your emotions aside.

QUESTION: What does "offer and acceptance" and "counter-offer" mean?

ANSWER: The "offer and acceptance" is the original contract written by the buyer to the seller—and, the purpose is to have the seller accept the offer, subject to certain terms and conditions. Most sellers have the terms already established with their listing bro-ker, and are hoping that a buyer will meet all of the conditions they want so that they can sell their home. In reality, most buyers do not have their "offer and acceptance" accepted on the first presentation. Most buyers want their selling agent to offer less than the seller wants, or they want some benefits that the seller will object to. If the seller rejects the "offer and acceptance," the contract is void and is no longer effective. If the seller does a "counter-offer" to the buyer's offer the counter is returned to the buyer's agent, to see if the buyer will agree to the added terms of the original offer. If the buyer accepts, then there is an agreeable contract, still subject to certain contingencies being met by all parties. Never lose a property sale over a few thousand dollars.

QUESTION: What does "earnest money" ("consideration") mean?

ANSWER: "Earnest money" is the good faith money deposited by the buyer under the terms of the purchase agreement contract, to be forfeited if the buyer defaults and applied to the purchase price if the sale is closed. Most "earnest money" deposits are put into an established escrow company account at the acceptance of the offer by the seller.

QUESTION: What does the word escrow mean?

ANSWER: The "escrow" company is basically a third party established to interpret the terms and conditions of the sale for all parties involved. The "escrow" (title and escrow) company is usually regulated by the state it is located in, and it is not allowed to give an opinion regarding the terms and conditions of the purchase agreement contract, but it can make sure everything is legal according to state law. The closing of a transaction is through this third party, the escrow agent who receives certain funds and documents to be delivered upon the performance of the specific conditions outlined in the escrow instructions. The escrow company is an unbiased third party.

QUESTION: What are "escrow instructions"?

ANSWER: "Escrow instructions" are the documents that set forth the duties of the escrow agent, as well as the requirements and obligations of all parties involved, when a transaction is closed through escrow.

QUESTION: What items does the escrow company need to complete their escrow, and close the transaction?

ANSWER: The escrow company will need the following items to complete their escrow:

- Copy of the "oOffer and Acceptance" (information about the sale)
- Earnest Money
- Copies of all Reports (Termite, Roof, Property Inspection)
- Loan Documents
- Original Documents Signed (Deed, Deed of Trust)
- Funds to Close the Escrow and Deliver the Deed

QUESTION: What does the lender do, and what are the different types of lenders?

ANSWER: The lender is the party who supplies the loan (money) to add to your proceeds to complete the transaction. You, the borrower, must qualify for the loan, and meet the conditions of the lender. The lender will secure their obligation on the property being purchased, with a deed of trust. The primary lender who loans his/her own money can be called a mortgage broker (institutional lender). The mortgage bankers are loan companies that originate, service, and sell loans to investors. The mortgage broker is an agent of the lender who brings the lender and borrower together. The mortgage broker shops his/her client around, for the best loan, and receives a fee for their service, if the loan records. The buyer/

borrower should shop around for the best rates, terms, and fees, when getting a loan to purchase a home. Remember, the property you are buying must appraise.

QUESTION: What are the normal costs of doing an escrow?

ANSWER: Normal costs vary from area-to-area, so I will talk about the most common costs for buyers and sellers when putting a real estate transaction together.

BUYER COSTS:
- Part of the Escrow Fee
- Document Fee
- Inspection Fee
- Recording Fee
- Transfer Tax Fee (portion)
- Lender Fees
- Title Insurance (Buyer, if any)
- Proration
- Homeowners Insurance

SELLER COSTS:
- Part of Escrow Fee
- Title Insurance (Owner's Policy)
- Document Fee
- Commission
- Recording
- Repairs
- Transfer Tax
- Proration

QUESTION: When does the buyer actually own the property?

ANSWER: Title to the property will be delivered to the buyer upon all parties signing the contract, escrow instructions, deed (seller), loan (buyer), and all monies being put in escrow. The normal trend is when the buyer has performed to the terms and conditions, the escrow agent will record the deed (or conveyance document), and deliver the funds to the seller, to close the transaction.

QUESTION: How does the seller get his/her funds?

ANSWER: The escrow agent, upon receiving all the funds and having all documents signed, will record the conveying document. Once the escrow agent has verification of the recording of the deed (conveyance of the document), in the county where the property is recorded, then the escrow agent will disburse funds to the seller, to complete the transaction.

QUESTION: How do real estate agents get paid?

ANSWER: Normally there are two agents involved in each transaction, one agent representing the buyer/purchaser, and one agent representing the seller. The buyer's agent is called the "selling agent" and the seller's agent is called the "listing agent." The seller normally pays the commission out of his/her sales proceeds at the close of escrow. Normally, a commission is 6% of the sales price, with 3% going to the buyer's broker, and 3% going to the seller's broker. Real estate agents do not get paid out of escrow; the broker receives the commissions and then disburses the amount owed to the agent from his/her own business account. In later sections I will explain the different types of agencies and how they affect you as a buyer or seller. Remember, all commissions are negotiable.

QUESTION: What information does a professional real estate agent need to know about the potential buyer that would make it easier for the buyer to achieve "home ownership?"

ANSWER: The following information will assist the real estate agent and allow them to be prepared to find you, the buyer the property that best suits your needs:

- Do you presently own a home, or have you owned a home?
- How much do you have available for a down payment?
- What is the source of the down payment?
- What town or city would you like to live in?
- What type of property do you prefer, home, condo, townhouse, or mobile home?
- What type of home do you want, single level, etc.?
- Do you need carpeting, a garage, or does it matter?
- How many bedrooms and bathrooms do you need?
- Do you need wheelchair access?
- How many people do you have in your household?
- Do you have pets?
- What are your needs regarding schools?
- Do you want to live near a shopping center?

If you supply all of this information to your Agent you will be much more successful and prepared to achieve your goal of "home ownership."

QUESTION: What information does your loan agent need to be able to qualify you, and obtain the best loan available for you, and your specific needs?

ANSWER: The average lender wants to be prepared so he/she will be able to qualify you for a loan. The loan process is two fold — first, the lender will have you, the buyer/borrower, fill out a loan application, run a credit report, and then, verify all documentation needed to validate your approval status. The lender can expedite the loan process if you, the borrower, are able to produce the following information, within a few days of your initial meeting with the loan agent:

- Job Information
- Gross Monthly Income
- Social Security Number
- Monthly Rent/Mortgage

- Checking/Savings Account balance
- Total Monthly Credit Payments
- Number of Children
- Childcare Monthly Expenses
- Monthly Child Support
- Have you ever filed Bankruptcy?
- Are you a Veteran?
- Date of Birth
- Two years of Federal Income Tax Statements
- Three months of Pay Stubs
- If self-employed, "Profit and Loss" of Business

All of this information will make your loan process go much faster, and will allow you some time to shop around for the best rates, before moving forward with the purchase of your "dream home."

This section will give you a better understanding of the process the buyer and seller must go through in the sale and purchase of real estate. We have determined, so far, that there are many types of real estate transactions, that it's better to own versus renting, and, finally, what takes place, if you do write an offer, and have it accepted.

Remember, the state of the economy predicts both the potential and the mind set of both the buyer and the seller.

CHAPTER FOUR

THE UPS AND DOWNS OF THE REAL ESTATE MARKET

Over the past twenty-five years, the local real estate market, as well as the national real estate market, has had its ups and downs. Traditionally, some areas are affected more than others.

What things affect the real estate market and cause it to go in a positive direction? Also, we must address what over the past twenty-five to thirty years has affected the economy and caused it to decline and create a negative affect on the real estate industry. Finally, how can the consumer who wants to buy or sell real estate change the way the current market is going?

It's always a better approach to start with the positive things that can and do affect the real estate market. The most obvious trend that will create an upswing in the market is supply and demand (basic economics). If people in your area want to purchase real estate, but the supply is limited, then prices will increase. To accent the supply/demand if interest rates and loan programs are good then home prices will go up. If the job market in the area where you live is good, and the potential growth factors are positive, then the housing values will be great.

Election years seem to stimulate the economy, because elected officials pass bills that either lower capital gains, introduce plans to give more tax benefits, or give exemptions for the sale of real estate. All these events will make values increase. Certain counties also allow home owners who are fifty-five years or older sell their personal residence, and transfer the low tax base to another home that qualifies. This could save someone a lot of money and prevent them from having to relocate to another area. And, things like the stock market, oil prices, the war, and the world economy will affect all aspects of the local real estate market.

On the downside, many things can affect the real estate market. Today's real estate market has been affected by the sub-prime loan problems. This has not only hurt the local market, but it has almost pushed the country into a recession with the mass losses of the larger loan companies.

The sub-prime mortgages that existed from 2006 to the present time, have put many properties into foreclosure, and created a downturn in the real estate market of up to a 40% loss in values. The stock market has declined – the dollar is at its lowest value in years – and many lenders have been forced to close their doors. Today's trends really have existed over the past twenty-five to thirty years and go in cycles until consumers change the negatives into positives through their spending habits.

Let's address the things that have happened over the past years that have hurt the economy. The pattern over the years has been constant — both buyer confidence level and lender confidence level is very low right now. Similar conditions in the real estate market have proved to be exceptional opportunities for investors who are able to take advantage of the market paralysis.

In the early 1970's, New York experienced the kind of hardships that caused the local market to stagnate and decrease in value. In 1973, the events leading to the disturbance in the market created a torrent that some buyers and sellers hated. The onset was the federal government's announcement of a moratorium on housing subsidies that had helped drive the market. Interest rates began to rise, making the cost of a mortgage more difficult to service. Inflation hit the market and the cost of doing business against short-term potential profit was a barrier. Just as in today's market, there was a drop in the value of the U.S. dollar.

By 1975, New York saw difficult lending practices and continued hardships. Most banks would not lend heavily because of the market outlook. In the summer of 1978, the levels of confidence rose again, and before the end of the year, property prices were on the rise once again, seeing healthy increases from 1978 through 1981, and beyond.

In 1980, the economy took a downturn and the affect on the real estate market caused interest rates to soar from 13% up to 18%. Investors accepted the fact that real estate was priced right, and I can tell you from personal experience that I was able to purchase three properties in Carson City, Nevada. For over three years, I rented out the properties, with a small negative, and in 1984, I was able to sell/exchange the properties and make a 50% profit over my initial investment. Remember when outside influences affect the normal way of dealing with real estate do not give up — there are alternative ways to help you turn a negative into a positive.

Another prime example in more recent years was during the time of the savings and loans scandals that affected the aerospace industry in California. With a loss of over 750,000 jobs in the State the housing scenario showed a sharp decline. In the following years, California began to see a recovery in the housing market followed by a boom thanks to extremely low interest rates. The "dot.com" bust also contributed to a shift in investment strategies. One could speculate that investors preferred real assets rather than a ghost opportunity here today and gone tomorrow.

In 1992, the Defense Department pulled out of California. This devastated the California economy and caused real estate values in the State to decline between 10-20%, which caused a ripple affect. I did some creative financing, and the clients that purchased property in 1993 not only profited, but are now Investors for me in other projects. If you buy right and hold onto the investment, the economy, over a 5-year swing, will correct itself.

Mix interest rates and a down market, with affordability on the rise, and a buyer's market will be created. The foreclosure and mortgage bank woes have not ended. There are good things on the horizon and consumer confidence is sure to regain strength before the end of 2009. New lender practices will be put in place and even though at the current time the loan industry is being conservative things will get better. New loan programs will be created and with that a better approach to real estate will take place.

The two examples that I have cited about New York and California represent two major areas that will created a major flow of the country. The current market will create some hardships but in the long run will also create opportunities for the Investor all across the country.

With the drastic changes in the real estate market consumers should recognize that times like these happen about once every couple of decades. As an investor/buyer you must position yourself to purchase properties with a creative exit plan in place. As a seller, even though your properties have declined and things are not looking good, you need to be able to analyze your situation and develop a new approach to your exit plan.

If you need to sell you can use the expertise of a company like the Equity Share Group to see if you can turn your present market negative into a positive by using a more creative approach. As a seller, the Equity Share Group can help you with creative approaches like a contract of sale, lease option, or possibly a supplemental program to get through your current situation with a profitable long-term goal. If you are an investor/seller the Equity Share Group can help you exchange out of a property you don't want into a better situation with a tenants-in-common interest.

The Equity Share Group predicts that between row and 2017 the real estate market outlook and prices will have climbed back to just below medium levels before the mortgage meltdown occurred. Things will get better and by making the move now you will have a profitable solution for the future.

CHAPTER FIVE

THE CONCEPT OF EQUITY SHARING/ JOINT OWNERSHIP

"Equity sharing" is a "creative" approach to real estate transactions, that links real estate investors with home buyers who can afford a monthly mortgage, but may not have enough cash for a full down payment. These two entities can be brought together with several benefits. The first benefit is that a buyer gets the opportunity to own a home and build up his/her own equity.

Secondly, the potential buyer's lack of cash, or cash-flow, prevented him/her from buying a home, but with "shared equity," he/she can use the money paid out in rent every month for house payments and enjoy the additional benefit of tax write-offs.

For investors a huge benefit is the rate of return on investment that exceeds return rates on mutual funds. Another benefit is the investor being able to invest in the real estate market without becoming a property manager. Finally, all investors look at the "equity sharing" approach as a great way to invest because of the many tax benefits. And, there are also ways to use IRA funds to invest in Real estate — however, specific regulations must be met.

Note that the concept of "equity sharing" will change with the ever-changing economic times.

HELPING OTHERS GET STARTED IN HOME OWNERSHIP

Equity haring is one way parents can help their children become first-time home buyers. It's also a great opportunity for baby boomers who need more money for retirement.

Someone else who might need equity sharing to achieve "home ownership" would be a newly divorced person who has lost half of the equity he/she had built up as part of a married couple. He/she may be able to make monthly mortgage payments but may not have the cash for a down payment. And, in some cases, he/she may also need help with monthly mortgage payments while waiting for the home to appreciate in value.

People who are relocating to the Bay Area, from a place where home prices were much lower, might also need an equity share partner, to be able to afford to get into the housing market. If they rent or lease for a year they will fall a year behind in investment opportunities, and also lose the tax advantages they would have had as a homeowner. Home prices in the Bay Area can be a culture shock to the reality of achieving "home ownership."

HOW EQUITY SHARE WORKS

The time period for an equity share agreement is usually three to five years, long enough for a home to show good appreciation in value, and give the home buyer time to refinance and pay off the investor. The equity split is generally 50/50. The amount of the split depends on each party's contribution to the initial investment, however, with today's economy, the time period will probably be five to seven years.

Generally, the Equity Share Group works with clients who are willing to invest $20,000 to $80,000 in a single property, or approximately 10% of the purchase price of the property. For example, an investor might invest $24,000, or 8%, in a home selling for $300,000, and the home Buyer would put in $8,000 to $10,000. The party who resides in the home would then pay the closing costs.

Most investors with the Equity Share Group turn their investments about three times within a ten-year time period — each time, investing in more properties. And the best part is that it's all tax free, if they keep reinvesting. Some Investors are choosing to sell off their rental apartments, and using the profits to invest in two or three homes, thus diversifying their investments. Investors with Starker, or 1031 Tax Exchanges, are frequently the ones who participate in this program.

Who can qualify to purchase a home through these methods?

The Equity Share Group counsels clients up front, and when they are pre-approved, we will begin showing them properties. About 90% of the clients who come to the Equity Share Group are able to use our programs.

While the idea may have seemed novel fifty-years-ago, a thirty-year loan wasn't very common, and now it's a fixture in the marketplace. Equity share agreements are proliferating the market providing more people with a way to participate in the housing market especially in the Bay Area.

In all cases a contract is drawn up, and specific terms and conditions are followed. Realtors often refer home buyers to the Equity Share Group, as a way of helping a buyer get into the home they want in the area they want to live in, affordably. Due to the current market trends and new FHA loan standards, a down payment of 3% might become the norm in the future.

CREATIVE WAYS TO ACHIEVE "HOME OWNERSHIP"

Equity sharing is a valid avenue to investing in the real estate market. The equity share concept usually works better in an economy where properties are more expensive and the market is slanted towards inflated values.

When your average down payment is approximately 10% of the purchase price and it takes a minimum of $22,000, or more, to get into a property, the equity share approach can help you achieve your goal. The first-time home buyer or the person who has to repair his/her credit is a perfect candidate for a "creative" method of buying real estate. Buyers who want a larger home than they can afford on their own might be able to accomplish their goal by approaching the seller with the possibility of doing an "equity share" as the investor for a portion of the equity in the property.

EXAMPLES OF ACTUAL "EQUITY SHARE/ JOINT OWNERSHIP" SITUATIONS

My first example of how successful the "Joint Ownership Program" has been, took place almost twenty years ago. In the early 1990s a young man came to me and asked me if I would sell his Hayward, California home so he could move into the San Ramon, California area. The new community was more expensive and he wanted to go from a small 1400 square foot home, to a larger 2300 square foot, 4 bedroom, 3 bathroom home. The problem was that, even though he had a good job and great credit, the down payment was $60,000, and he only had $20,000 from the sale of his home.

The owner of a beautiful home in San Ramon, California had not been able to sell his home the conventional way so I approached him about the concept of doing an "equity share/joint ownership" with my buyer. The sales price was $300,000, and the down payment would be shared with $20,000 coming from the buyer and $40,000 left in the property by the seller.

The "joint ownership agreement" was set up for three to five years, with the buyer/occupant getting the new loan and paying for all of the expenses of owning the property. At some point, the buyer/occupant would then buy out the investor/seller with the equity contributed, plus a percentage of the upside equity growth in the home, over the five years. The economy in California was in a decline from 1992 through 1997, but the investor was eventually bought out with his initial $60,000, plus an upside growth of an additional $65,000, which was a tremendous return.

The owner/buyer still owns the property, and the home value has gone up from the initial $300,000 to $850,000. In 2004, my owner/buyer became an investor and has since contributed over $150,000 into various joint ownerships doubling his returns. "Equity share/joint ownerships" work but you must do things in the right way. Be aware of property values, never risk all your investment money in Real estate, and finally, be sure to work with someone who understands the market and your specific goals.

The second example of how an "equity share/joint ownership" works is a standard profile. A young couple with a little girl was renting an apartment in Berkeley, California. Their rent was about $1,200 a month, but they wanted to have the stability of owning a home. My wife, BJ, a Real estate Agent, agreed to do an equity share with them, so that they could get into a condo development. Their condo was 1,200 square feet with 2 bedrooms, and 1 bathroom, and was conveniently located near shopping and Bay Area Rapid Transit (BART).

With a 10% down payment, they were able to get a 90% loan, with payments of $850 per month, condo fees of $100, and property taxes of $300 a month. So, for only $1,250 a month, they had achieved home ownership and had approximately $18,000 in tax write-offs, per year. Three years later they sold their condo for $290,000, paid back the investor, and purchased a home in Berkeley, California for $500,000, where they live today. Equity sharing helped them save their eventual down payment, got them into the home of their dreams, and created the best possible situation for their family. It would have taken this couple at least ten years to save up a down payment to get started into the housing market, and they would have been throwing away their hard earned money on rent all that time.

My "equity share program" accelerated their dream and allowed them to achieve their desired goal much sooner than they ever thought possible.

My "equity share/joint ownership program" does not always work because even couples who want to own the home they're trying to purchase violate the contract due to the economy, job loss, or other family crisis circumstances beyond their control.

The investor is almost always willing to extend the agreement time period, or work out a different approach to help achieve a successful outcome for all parties involved. If the buyer/occupant decides to walk away from their commitment, the investor has the right to either foreclose or take legal action to protect his/her investment. My company, the Equity Share Group, has always taken the position that we will act as the facilitator/mediator so that all parties have a chance to perform, or find an alternative way to live up to a contract.

In the current economy, where property values have declined 30% to 50%, investors and buyers often have no alternative but to extend their contracts. The only way an "equity share/joint ownership" can work is if all parties have enough flexibility to adapt.

Let's define what equity sharing is and how it affects the owner/investor, the potential buyer, and any and all other parties who may be involved in the transaction.

What does the concept of equity share mean?

The "equity share" approach to real estate has been around for many years, but not in the formal structure that now exists. Relatives, usually parents and their children, have been involved in situations where the parent lends his/her child the down payment for a home, and hopes to, some day, have a return on the investment. In the more formal approach, you place the occupant/resident into a property of his/her choice. The occupant/resident and the investor must form a "joint partnership" as to their ownership in the property and what benefits they will get out of their venture. The investor will help with a part of the down payment, while the owner/resident is responsible for making all the payments and taking care of the property.

Who are the parties that make up the "equity share" concept?

Many parties are involved in an actual equity share concept and transaction. The first party is the owner/resident. This party wants to own a home and needs assistance in some form to be able to achieve his/her goal. The owner/resident knows that they will be responsible for the monthly payments, upkeep of property, insurance, and any problems that might surface during the equity share contract timeframe. The owner/investor is the party who is not going to live in the property but is involved in the arrangement for investment purposes only. The owner/investor will put up some of the down payment, will share in capital improvements and will be able to declare some of the tax write-offs. The other parties to the concept will be discussed in later questions.

Does the Internal Revenue Service (IRS) recognize the equity share concept?

The IRS will allow a non-resident investor to make the down payment, and the owner/resident to pay the monthly expenses. The IRS Code is 280A, and all of the paper work, and structure, must be done the right way, to be qualified as a valid equity share contract. You might check with a CPA who works with a real property attorney for making sure that this is set up correctly.

What are the benefits to the owner/resident under the equity share agreement?

The owner/resident is the party who will occupy the property as a permanent residence. The benefits that are needed to make it worthwhile for the owner/resident are the following:

a.   The owner/resident has the opportunity to acquire a home with little or no down payment.

b.   The owner/resident will receive income tax benefits for a part of the mortgage interest, and the property taxes. This benefit equates to thousands of dollars in savings.

c.   The owner/resident will receive an agreed-upon percentage of the net profits once the property is sold. We encourage all owner/residents to buy out the owner/investors.

d.   The owner/resident by doing an equity share has the opportunity to live in a larger home with more favorable terms.

e.   Finally, the owner/resident has the potential to buy out the owner/investor and receive full ownership.

What are the benefits to the owner/investor under the equity share agreement?

The owner/investor is really a passive owner of a portion of a property and treats the property as a rental. The benefits to the owner/investor are:

a.   The owner/investor by doing the equity share will own a part of the property; hopefully that investment will grow in equity (profit on sale).

b.   The owner/investor will receive tax benefits, such as depreciation, property taxes, improvements, and a portion of the interest — all without the worry of the property management.

c.   The owner/investor will have few maintenance problems and does not need to concern his/herself with property value declining due to upkeep as there is no direct property management.

d.   Finally, the owner/investor can create greater leverage with his/her investment dollars, without the risk, and still preserve his/her tax advantages. The tax savings through 1031 Tax Exchanges are crucial to the owner/investor who needs to diversify.

What is an equity share contract?

The equity share contract/agreement is a meeting of the minds between the owner/resident and the owner/investor. All the terms and conditions must be understood and agreed upon.

What provisions does the IRS, Code 280A, require to be contained in the equity share contract/agreement?

The IRS makes it clear that it will only accept the equity share contract/agreement if it contains the following:

    a.   Title ownership of all parties (investors and residents)

    b.   Names of all co-owners and their percentages of ownership

    c.   The buy-out arrangements that exist between all parties

    d.   Provisions for the profit split, if needed

    e.   Arbitration of any disputes that might arise

    f.   Payment of capital improvements

    g.   There must be provisions for payment of any extra ordinary costs

    h.   A Fair Rental Agreement for the owner/investor's ownership (offset)

    i.   The timeframe of the agreement

What makes up the terms and conditions of the equity share contract/agreement?

The equity share contract/agreement and its conditions are extremely important to the overall understanding of the entire contract/agreement. The contract/agreement, along with the memorandum, the escrow instructions, and the "offer and acceptance," informs all parties as to what must be done to have a valid contract/agreement.

The following terms and conditions must be implemented into the equity share contact/agreement:

    a.   The terms of the agreement (years, sales price, down payment, etc.)

b. Vesting, how the parties will hold title

c. The mortgage (loan), and which party is responsible for paying the monthly obligation

d. The repair obligation and how it's defined

e. The default conditions

f. The distribution of profits

g. Tax benefits and how they are to be disbursed

h. The buy-out contingencies

i. Miscellaneous items, such as, divorce, death or bankruptcy

j. The contract extension, if any

k. Insurance

l. Assignment

m. Selling expenses or cost of sale

What approach should you use to market the equity share concept?

When a real estate broker/agent is looking for property that might qualify for the equity share approach he/she must look at the following to put the content together:

- Investors who are doing 1031 Tax Exchanges make perfect investors for equity share transactions. Investors are able to diversify their investment, do more transactions than they could on their own, and get all of the benefits of owning an investment property, without the problems of property management. No loans are usually in the Investor's name.

- All first-time home buyers are candidates for an equity share. The new homeowner usually does not have enough down payment or must move so far from where they work that "home ownership" is not worth while. The investor can help the first-time home buyer into his/her first property. Parents often become the investors on an equity share with their children, because it's a great way to help them.

- Owners/residents who have bad credit can become good prospects for the "equity share program."

- Transfers from other areas make good potential owners/residents because they usually have culture shock when they see prices of homes compared to the areas where they have lived.

- Property owners with difficult homes to sell may consider putting their homes on the market under the "equity share program."

- Senior homeowners might consider becoming an investor with his/her property by carrying back the down payment so they can get the tax benefits, and make it easier to sell the home.

How can the owner/resident profit by using the "equity share program"?

The owner/resident can profit in two ways, when it comes to participating in an equity share arrangement. First of all, the owner/resident gets to live in the home of his/her dreams, without having to save up the 20% down payment to purchase the home. Secondly, the owner/resident gets tax benefits that will save thousands of dollars a year compared to the typical renter. Finally, the owner/resident will either buy out the investor and live in the property for several years or will sell with the investor and keep a percentage of his/her profits for reinvestment.

What rights does the owner/resident usually have when they exercise their option?

The owner/resident can do one of two things when it comes to exercising their rights to "home ownership" under the equity share approach. First, the owner/resident can buy out the investor at market value, appraised value, or agreed upon value. The owner/resident will be credited for his/her down payment, plus principal reduction of the loan, and then add in a percentage of the profits, after costs, that has been agreed upon in the contract. Second, the owner/resident can sell with the investor, and share in the profits, based on his/her percentage.

Instead of an outside investor participating in the equity share arrangement, can the seller/owner of the property become the investor?

Yes. And, this will happen more frequently in a buyer's market. The seller has a real potential to profit and make the sale of his/her property easier than the normal transaction.

In a soft market, the seller usually has a hard time moving his/her property. The seller can take advantage of the equity share approach, and sell a portion of the property — and retain a percentage of the property as an investment. The additional benefits are as follows:

    a.   The seller/investor is really investing in a property that he/she is very familiar with.

    b.   The seller/investor can save thousands of dollars because the investor only has to transfer a percentage of his/her base for tax reasons.

    c.   The seller/investor will not have to worry about a negative cash flow, or property management, in regards to his/her investment portion of the property.

    d.   The seller/investor, upon the sale of the remaining portion of the property (investment), can do a 1031 Tax Exchange with the value, and save tax dollars. The seller/investor will not have to reinvest in a larger property, but will only have to match up to their percentage value.

    e.   Finally, the property in question is much easier to market doing an "equity share," and the value that the seller will receive will be more to market price.

What are the lender requirements when pre-qualifying a buyer who is doing an equity share arrangement with an investor?

Lenders, in general, really do not understand the equity share concept. They usually want all parties that are going to be on title to the property, to also be on the loan. I feel that lenders should be required to keep pace with the market and understand that, if you have a borrower (owner/resident), who has good credit, job security, adequate income, and all they lack is the required down payment, then there must be a way to get them a loan. The "equity share program" would allow the owner/resident to put down 5% of the down payment and have the owner/investor put down the remaining 5% to 10% and use the owner/resident qualifications to get the loan.

The following requirements are needed by the gender for them to consider the equity share arrangement:

a. The owner/resident must live in the property.

b. The owner/resident must be able to pay the mortgage payment.

c. The property taxes and insurance can be split or allocated.

d. The equity share agreement must be prepared and accepted by the lender, or done outside of escrow.

e. The owner/investor does not have to qualify for the income.

f. The lender will not usually make over an 80% loan to value (LTV).

g. The owner/resident must have at least 5% of his/her own money.

The new FHA loan programs will fit the equity share program with a 3% down payment.

How can the owner/investor profit from the equity share arrangement?

When the investor buys a property under the "equity share program" they are able to create greater leverage than is possible with buying a rental home on their own.

The lender usually requires the investor in a rental home to put at least 20% cash down into the rental property. However, with the "equity share program" the investor is often able to buy with 10% owner occupied financing. When this type of financing is unavailable the Investor is able to buy with the same 20% down required in a rental.

With an equity share property the investor contractually obligates another party to pay 100% of the negative cash flow. This investment further extends the investor's leverage into the property. The investor shares the future appreciation of the property with the occupant owner. The investor will get tax benefits, return of investment and finally, a chance to extend their base to more properties.

What are the tax benefits to the owner/resident?

The usual tax benefits to the owner/resident will be the interest write-off, the property tax write-off, and some capital improvements, if agreed upon.

What are the benefits for the owner/investor?

The tax benefits to the owner/investor will usually be the following: some interest write-off (if arranged), depreciation, repairs, property taxes (if agreed upon), and finally the right to do a 1031 Tax Exchange if a sale takes place.

How does the equity share concept affect a real estate broker/agent and how can it be profitable?

The real estate broker/agent should become aware of different approaches to buying and selling real estate. I have made a good living by helping buyers and investors use the equity share concept to profit in the real estate market. A realtor who has a buyer with good credit and a good job, but lacks the down payment money, should not give up on his/her client. Instead, he/she should either find an investor (could be a family member, or an outside investor), or find a seller who is willing to equity share his/her home, and put the transaction together.

Most of my clients have been investors coming out of 1031 Tax Exchanges, and they need to reinvest. I've been able to find them four investments by equity sharing versus one investment the conventional way. It's easy to find a buyer/resident who can invest 5% of his/her own money to live in a nice home, and have the potential to profit. My advice to agents is, use your "creative" mind, and always look at alternative ways to help your clients buy or sell real estate. Remember that investors are also able to make contributions out of their IRAs (loans).

How can I protect my investor/client when he/she invests in an equity share contract?

The investor can't really default when involved in the equity share process. The investor must protect his/her equity, if the owner/resident fails to live up to his/her portion of the contract. There are a few methods that the investor can take action against the owner/resident, if the agreement is violated.

1. All equity share agreements have a note and deed of trust, created between the owner/resident and the owner/investor for the investor's equity. The deed of trust can only be foreclosed against if a violation has occurred. The foreclosure process usually takes approximately 120-days (non-judicial foreclosure).

2. The resident and the investor can draw up an agreement to sell the property. This is a separate document, allowing the investor to put the property on the market at the expense of the resident.

3. The investor could establish a "quiet title" action but a lawyer would have to be contacted.

4. The investor is named as an additional insured party on the policy. The investor also gets monthly updates on mortgage payments and tax installments.

WHAT TO LOOK FOR IN AN EQUITY SHARE AGREEMENT/CONTRACT

First, an equity share agreement/contract should ALWAYS be in writing. Both the owner/investor and the owner/occupant are both on the title to the residence and any agreements between them should be in writing.

The agreement should always clearly identify the parties involved, their internal relationships (i.e. husband and wife), and their relationship to each other (i.e. investor is an owner of an undivided 50% interest as a tenant-in-common). The agreement should spell out, specifically, who is to pay what, at what time, and to whom. It should also specifically cover who maintains and repairs the property and what happens if either one of the parties wants to add a capital addition (like a swimming pool) to the property. Also a major item (such as a heater or roof) going out that necessitates capital improvements to the property which are not simple repairs or maintenance must be covered in this written agreement.

The property should be clearly identified and the ownership percentages of that property spelled out. The agreement should state what happens upon the death of the owner/investor or the owner/occupant, what happens if either party files for bankruptcy, has his/her assets put under a lien or just simply disappears. The default provisions should clearly protect both parties and give them remedies in the event of a default on the other party's part.

Equally important, the written document should provide that, upon the end of the equity sharing term, the owner/occupant has the opportunity to buy out the owner/investor. This is primary since the owner/occupant has put down "roots" in the residence and should have the first right to purchase the owner/investor's interest. Failing that, the owner/investor should have the right to purchase the interest of the owner/occupant and if neither wishes to purchase the property the property is put on the open market and sold to a third party.

How are the interests of the other party valued at the time of such a purchase? This important provision should be in any equity sharing agreement. Of course, the "boiler plate" provision that protects both parties (i.e. a clause providing where and how disputes are to be settled) should be in the written document.

These contracts sound like they are long and comprehensive—and they are! Every clause, however, is carefully drafted and designed to protect the rights of both parties, and to ensure that the owner/investor, and the owner/occupant, each obtain the full benefits from the equity sharing relationship. Ownership splits must be agreed upon before the final contract is signed.

In conclusion, the aspect of "equity sharing" is to make the housing market available to as many potential "home-owners" as possible. The first-time home buyer usually does not have enough money saved to put the down payment on a property. The equity share approach allows a benefit to both the owner/occupant and the owner/investor. It also opens up new avenues to the real estate broker/agent who wants to make a difference in making the "AMERICAN DREAM" come true. Always look to the professional who understands the concept of equity share to assist you in your next transaction.

EQUITY SHARE AGREEMENT PARAMETERS

Joint Ownership

- Owner/Occupant
- Investor/Owner

Items That Make Up the Equity Share Agreement

1. Time Period
2. Contribution
3. Maintenance
4. Insurance
5. Capital Improvements and Compensation
6. Security and Default (Investor Documents)
7. Fair Market Value Buy-out (Determination)
8. Co-operation in a 1031 Tax Exchange
9. Right of First Refusal
10. Options at End of Term
11. Distribution of Proceeds
12. Transfer
13. Indemnity
14. Reimbursement
15. Write-offs (Taxes)
16. Fair Rental Agreement (Active Investor)
17. Heirs
18. Attorney Fees
19. Disclosures

EQUITY SHARE AGREEMENT DOCUMENTATION

Active Investor – Example: 1031 Tax Exchange

1. Deed
2. Deed of Trust and Note
3. Memorandum of Joint Ownership
4. Equity Share Co-Tenancy Agreement
5. Fair Rental Agreement
6. Escrow Instructions
7. Purchase Agreement and Disclosures
8. Exchange Documentation if Needed
9. Closing Statement
10. Title Insurance
11. Servicing Agreement

In-Active Investor – Example: Self-Directed IRA (PENSCO). Investors using money from IRAs do not have property ownership rights. Their investment is a secured loan with a beneficiary.

1. Deed of Trust
2. Note – Participating
3. Agreement
4. Escrow Instructions
5. Title Instructions
6. Servicing Agreement

EXAMPLES OF TYPICAL EQUITY SHARE PROGRAM SCENARIOS FOR A BUYER:

- You qualify for FHA financing for a 97% loan.

- You have been pre-approved for 90-95% financing but the payments are too high.

- You have been pre-approved for 90-95% financing but the purchase price you qualify for is too low to purchase the home you want.

- You can qualify for 90-95% financing but you don't have money for the down payment.

- You have 10% of your own money but due to bad credit you can only qualify for 80% financing.

- You own a home now, and want to upgrade to another home but you can't afford the monthly payments.

- You own a home now and want to buy a rental property but you don't have enough equity.

- You are getting a divorce and want to buy a home on your own but don't want to use up all of your cash.

EQUITY SHARE PROGRAM DOCUMENTS:

1. MEMORANDUM OF JOINT OWNERSHIP AGREEMENT

MEMORANDUM OF JOINT OWNERSHIP AGREEMENT

This Memorandum of Joint Ownership Agreement is intended to provide notice that, _____, vesting (Owner/Occupant), and _____, vesting (Owner/Investor), have entered into an Agreement effective Month Day, Year with respect to the certain Real Property, commonly known as Address, City, CA, with legal description of which is set forth in <u>Exhibit A</u>, hereto.

This Joint Ownership Agreement is effective as of the date on which the property becomes vested in the parties as Tenants-in-Common, and shall continue until the interest of one or both parties is sold, or Owner/Occupant exercises his or her buyout option as provided in the Co-Tenancy Agreement.

Except, as otherwise provided in the Joint Ownership Agreement, no party may assign, sell, transfer, hypothecate, or otherwise alienate any portion of his or her interest in the property or the Co-Tenancy Agreement, without the prior written consent of the other party. This Joint Ownership Agreement will terminate on Month Day, Year, unless extended by all parties.

Owner/Occupant   Dated

_____   _____
Name

_____   _____
Name

Owner/Investor   Dated

_____   _____
Name

_____   _____
Name

Date _____

State of California
County of _____

On _____
Before me, _____, a Notary Public,
personally appeared _____,
who proved to me on the basis of satisfactory evidence to be the person(s) whose name(s) is/are subscribed to the within instrument and acknowledged to me that he/she/they executed the same in his/her/their authorized capacity(ies), and that by his/her/their signature(s) on the instrument the person(s) or the entity upon behalf of which the person(s) acted, executed the instrument.

I certify under PENALTY OF PERJURY under the laws of the State of California that the foregoing paragraph is true and correct.

WITNESS my hand and official seal.

_____
Signature

Sample Document

2. EQUITY SHARE CO-TENANCY AGREEMENT OF JOINT OWNERSHIP (1 OF 11 PAGES)

EQUITY SHARE CO-TENANCY AGREEMENT OF JOINT OWNERSHIP

THIS AGREEMENT is entered into and effective as of Month Day, Year, by _____, vesting, ("OWNER/OCCUPANT"), on the one hand, and _____, vesting, ("OWNER/INVESTOR"), on the other hand.

OWNER/INVESTOR and OWNER/OCCUPANT are to take title to that certain residential property, commonly known as _____, City, CA ("Property"). The parties wish to enter into an agreement regarding the ownership, management, and disposition of the PROPERTY. Therefore, in consideration of the mutual promises contained in the Agreement, the parties hereby agree as follows:

1. **TERMS OF AGREEMENT AND EXTENSION:** This Co-Tenancy Agreement is effective as of the date set forth above, and said Agreement shall continue in effect for a period of three (3) years from the date of closing, at which time this Agreement shall be terminated in accordance with Section 17. Alternatively, the parties may extend the terms of this Agreement for an additional two (2) years, by written mutual consent of the parties.

2. **MANNER OF HOLDING TITLE:** The parties shall hold title to the PROPERTY as Tenants-in-Common, with the OWNER/INVESTOR owning an undivided 0% interest and the OWNER/OCCUPANT owning an undivided 0% interest.

3. **OWNER/INVESTOR CONTRIBUTION:** The parties mutually agree that the fair market value of the property, as of the date of this Agreement, is $000,000.00. Upon acquisition of the PROPERTY, by the parties, the PROPERTY will be subject to a new Deed of Trust loan in the sum of approximately $000,000.00. OWNER/INVESTOR initial contribution will be $ _____ towards the down payment of the purchase of the PROPERTY.

4. **OWNER/OCCUPANT CONTRIBUTION:** Owner/Occupant agrees to make the following contribution to the PROPERTY:

   A. OWNER/OCCUPANT will pay all loan payments, property taxes, and insurance regarding the PROPERTY. OWNER/OCCUPANT shall provide proof to OWNER/INVESTOR, each month, that all of these payments are current.

   B. OWNER/OCCUPANT will pay for all costs of repairs or maintenance on the PROPERTY.

   C. OWNER/OCCUPANT will use their 0% interest in the PROPERTY for a primary residence.

1

Sample Document

EQUITY SHARE CO-TENANCY AGREEMENT OF JOINT OWNERSHIP (2 OF 11 PAGES)

5. **DOCUMENTATION:** The Equity Share transaction between OWNER/ INVESTOR and the OWNER/OCCUPANT will be evidenced by the following documents, each of which is an integral part of the entire transaction between the parties:

    A. This Equity Share Co-Tenancy Agreement Of Joint Ownership ("Agreement");

    B. The Addendum Fair Rental Agreement To Joint Ownership Agreement ("Addendum"), which Addendum is attached hereto and incorporated herein;

    C. The Agreement To Purchase between the OWNER/INVESTOR and OWNER/OCCUPANT ("Purchase Agreement"), a copy of which is attached hereto and incorporated herein;

    D. Grant Bargain Sale Deed

    E. Deed of Trust With Assignment of Rents (Deed of Trust) and Note

    F. Memorandum of Joint Ownership Agreement

    G. Exchange Documentation (if needed)

6. **MAINTENANCE:** OWNER/OCCUPANT will be solely responsible for maintaining the PROPERTY and for paying for all the costs of all everyday repairs to the PROPERTY. OWNER/OCCUPANT hereby covenants to keep, and maintain, and repair the property in good condition so as to enhance its value.

7. **INSURANCE:** OWNER/OCCUPANT will purchase and maintain a valid homeowner's insurance policy from an insurance company of their choice. OWNER/OCCUPANT will be responsible for all insurance premiums and deductibles. OWNER/INVESTORS will be named on the insurance policy as an "additional insured" to protect their equity in the property.

    A. **Home Insurance:** The homeowner's insurance, that the OWNER/ OCCUPANT will provide, will provide for full replacement cost of the dwelling, with a deductible not to exceed $1,000.00. In the event of a total loss, the proceeds of such homeowner's insurance policy, after payment to the holder of the First Deed of Trust on the PROPERTY, shall be allocated among the parties in the same manner as is provided upon the sale of the PROPERTY. The cost of paying the deductible, in case of an insurance claim, will be the OWNER/OCCUPANT'S responsibility.

    B. **Liability Insurance:** OWNER/OCCUPANT will obtain liability insurance coverage in an amount of, not less than Five Hundred

Sample Document

EQUITY SHARE CO-TENANCY AGREEMENT OF JOINT OWNERSHIP (3 OF 11 PAGES)

Thousand Dollars ($500,000.00), either in conjunction with a homeowner's insurance policy, and /or umbrella policy.

8. CAPITAL IMPROVEMENTS:

A. OWNER/OCCUPANT shall not make capital improvements over $3,000.00 without the prior written consent of the OWNER/INVESTOR. OWNER/OCCUPANT shall not be compensated or receive credit for capital improvements, unless prior written consent of the OWNER/INVESTOR is obtained.

B. All improvements, or structural changes, must be done according to local building codes, with applicable permits, and using licensed and properly insured contractors. All improvements must be agreed upon, in writing, by all parties.

9. COMPENSATION FOR CAPITAL IMPROVEMENTS:
OWNER/OCCUPANT will be compensated for capital improvements they make to the PROPERTY, pursuant to Section 8 supra, in the form of a credit at time of buyout, under this Agreement, or when the PROPERTY is sold jointly by the parties and the proceeds of the sale are distributed pursuant to Section 18 of this Agreement, according to the following conditions:

A. Compensation will be based on the actual appreciated value caused by the improvements as determined by licensed appraiser within 2 months after completion. The cost of the appraiser shall be split evenly by the parties. Alternatively, the parties may agree in writing to the actual value, instead of using an appraiser.

B. Actual appreciated value shall be determined by a licensed appraiser who will be chosen by mutual agreement of the OWNER/OCCUPANT and OWNER/INVESTOR;

C. OWNER/OCCUPANT shall inform OWNER/INVESTOR when improvements have been completed;

D. Compensation shall be made only at the time of buyout or distribution of the proceeds of the joint sale of the PROPERTY pursuant to Section 18 of this Agreement.

10. ENCUMBRANCES AND ASSIGNMENTS:

A. The OWNER/OCCUPANT cannot assign this Agreement, or transfer their ownership interest in the PROPERTY, in whole or in part, without the written consent of the OWNER/INVESTOR, which consent shall not be withheld unreasonably. This Agreement may be assigned by the OWNER/INVESTOR. The OWNER/INVESTOR also have the option

3

Sample Document

EQUITY SHARE CO-TENANCY AGREEMENT OF JOINT OWNERSHIP (4 OF 11 PAGES)

of assigning this Joint Ownership Agreement due to a future Exchange. The parties acknowledge, by signing this Agreement, that if assignment takes place, it will be under the existing Terms and Conditions.

B. Notwithstanding Provision 10.A., OWNER/INVESTOR or OWNER/OCCUPANT may transfer their ownership interest, in whole or in part, to a Spouse, a Lineal Descendent, or a Trust, for their benefit, and such transfer shall be deemed reasonable and consented to under Section 10.A. of this Agreement.

C. Under Proposition 13, the OWNER/OCCUPANT will be obliged to pay any increased property tax assessment attributable to the sale or transfer, where applicable.

D. Neither the OWNER/OCCUPANT nor the OWNER/INVESTOR shall obtain a loan secured by their respective interest in the PROPERTY during the term of this Agreement, without the written consent of the other party.

E. Neither the OWNER/OCCUPANT nor the OWNER/INVESTOR shall Allow an involuntary lien (such as a Federal or State Tax Lien, or a Judgment) to be placed on their respective ownership interests in the PROPERTY.

F. OWNER/OCCUPANT may rent a room(s) in the PROPERTY, but must Indemnify the OWNER/INVESTOR for any damage to the PROPERTY or liability for injury.

G. If the OWNER/OCCUPANT dies, their heirs will have the right to maintain this Agreement by performing the OWNER/OCCUPANT'S duties under this Agreement. If the OWNER/OCCUPANT'S heirs fail, or refuse, to perform the OWNER/OCCUPANT'S duties under this Agreement, then the PROPERTY shall be sold pursuant to Sections 16, 17, 18, and 19 of this Agreement. IF the OWNER/INVESTOR dies, then this Agreement will stay in existence, according to its Terms and Conditions.

H. Demand Note to Protect Investor's Interest. OWNER/OCCUPANT agrees to execute a Demand Promissory Note and Deed of Trust with Assignment of Rents in the amount of ($ 0.00) secured by his/her interest in the property (see exhibit), for the purpose of securing the OWNER/INVESTOR (investment) equity capital account, establishing the minimum redemption price. In addition, said redemption shall include but not be limited by, any penalties, legal and closing costs, foreclosure costs, incurred by OWNER/INVESTOR that may have been expended as a consequence of the default of the other during the term of this Agreement

4

Sample Document

EQUITY SHARE CO-TENANCY AGREEMENT OF JOINT OWNERSHIP (5 OF 11 PAGES)

11. DEFAULT: The occurrence of any of the following shall constitute a default by the OWNER/OCCUPANT or OWNER/INVESTOR:

    A. Failure to make any payment, when due, as required under this Agreement, and such failure continues for thirty (30) calendar days after notice has been given to the defaulting party.

    B. Assigning this Agreement or transferring their ownership in the PROPERTY in violation of Section 10.A. of this agreement.

    C. Obtaining a loan secured by the PROPERTY without the written permission of the other party.

    D. Allowing an involuntary lien(s) to be placed on their respective interest in the PROPERTY, and failing to remove the lien within sixty (60) days after notice has been given to the defaulting party.

    E. Abandonment of, or failure to, occupy the PROPERTY for sixty (60) consecutive days without proper notification and maintenance.

    F. Willful or negligent damage to the PROPERTY.

    G. Failure to keep property taxes current.

    H. Failure to keep required limits of hazard insurance current.

    I. Failing to perform, or breaching, any obligation of this Agreement, the Addendum the Purchase Agreement or the Deed of Trust which the OWNER/OCCUPANT or OWNER/INVESTOR are obligated to perform.

12. REMEDIES: OWNER/INVESTOR and OWNER/OCCUPANT shall have the following remedies, in the event of default as set forth in Section 11 of this Agreement. These remedies are not exclusive, and are in addition to any remedies now or later permitted by law and equity, including, but not limited to, specific performance.

    A. FORCLOSURE: OWNER/INVESTOR may Foreclose upon their Deed of Trust on OWNER/OCCUPANT'S ownership interest in the PROPERTY. Such Foreclosure may be either Judicial Foreclosure or Non-Judicial Foreclosure.

        1. Foreclosure, In The Event Of OWNER/OCCUPANT'S Monetary Default: If the OWNER/OCCUPANT'S default relates to their failure to pay money to anyone, including, but not limited to, the holder of the First Deed

5

Sample Document

EQUITY SHARE CO-TENANCY AGREEMENT OF JOINT OWNERSHIP (6 OF 11 PAGES)

of Trust holder on the PROPERTY, or for property taxes or insurance on the PROPERTY, the OWNER/INVESTOR may, but is not obligated to, advance the money necessary to the third party, to pay the amount owing and commence a Foreclosure proceeding, to enforce the amount so advanced against the OWNER/OCCUPANT plus any other sums so advanced during the course of the Foreclosure proceeding.

2. **Foreclosure, In Event Of OWNER/OCCUPANT'S Non-Monetary Default:** If the OWNER/OCCUPANT'S default relates to their failing to perform, or their breaching any obligation of this Agreement, the Addendum, the Purchase Agreement or the Deed of Trust which obligation to pay money, including, but not limited to, the OWNER/OCCUPANT'S failure or refusal to comply with and/or perform their obligations under Sections 16, 17, or 18 of this Agreement, then OWNER/OCCUPANT and OWNER/INVESTOR agree that it would be difficult and impractical to determine, at the time of this Agreement, the exact amount of monetary damages that the OWNER/INVESTORS would sustain, and the parties therefore agree that in the event of such default by the OWNER/OCCUPANT, the OWNER/INVESTOR will be entitled to liquidated damages in the sum of $0.00, which is the approximate amount of the OWNER/INVESTOR'S initial contribution to acquire the PROPERTY, plus a 0% simple interest, per annum, accruing from the date of acquisition of the PROPERTY.

3. **Foreclosure Procedures Set Forth Above Are Not Exclusive:** Subject to provision 12.A.4. below, the Foreclosure procedures set forth in Sections 12.A.1 and 2 above, are not exclusive of any other Foreclosure procedures that the OWNER/INVESTOR may use. The OWNER/INVESTOR may utilize Judicial Foreclosure procedures, or Non-Judicial Foreclosure procedures, that they are entitled to use by statute, law or equity, in addition to, and/or different from, the procedures set forth in Sections 12.A.1 and 2 above.

4. **Notice Of OWNER/INVESTORS' Election to Foreclose:** If the OWNER/INVESTORS elect to exercise their Foreclosure Remedy described herein, the OWNER/INVESTORS' must first send by certified mail a written notice of default to the Owner/Occupant at the address of the PROPERTY describing the Terms and Conditions

6

Sample Document

EQUITY SHARE CO-TENANCY AGREEMENT OF JOINT OWNERSHIP (7 OF 11 PAGES)

of this Agreement that are in default. Thirty (30) days after mailing said notice, the investor may cause commence either a Judicial or Non-Judicial Foreclosure proceeding concerning the PROPERTY.

B. EXERCISE OF BUY-OUT RIGHTS: In the event that either the OWNER/OCCUPANT or the OWNER/INVESTOR default in any of their obligations under this Agreement, the Addendum, the Purchase Agreement, or the Deed of Trust, and the nature of default is such that it cannot reasonably be cured by the defaulting party, then the non-defaulting party may exercise their buyout rights under Sections 16, 17, and 18 of this Agreement.

C. LEGAL ACTION: The OWNER/INVESTOR may take legal action in Court (including, but not limited to, a Quiet Title action) to obtain the OWNER/OCCUPANT'S interest in the PROPERTY.

13. PENALTIES AND LATE CHARGES: Both parties acknowledge that, if OWNER/OCCUPANT or the OWNER/INVESTOR does not make any payment when due under the terms of Section 4, and the OWNER/INVESTOR advances the payment, the OWNER/INVESTOR will thereby incur various costs, the exact amount of which is difficult and impractical to fix. Accordingly, in addition to reimbursing the OWNER/INVESTOR for any amount the so advance, the OWNER/OCCUPANT hereby agrees to pay the OWNER/INVESTOR damages in the sum of eight percent (8%) of the amount that the OWNER/INVESTOR advanced.

14. CO-OPERATION IN A SECTION 1031 EXCHANGE: Upon the sale of the OWNER/INVESTORS' share of the PROPERTY, the OWNER/OCCUPANT agrees to cooperate at no expense to the OWNER/OCCUPANT.

15. FAIR MARKET VALUE: For the purpose of the right of first refusal described In Section 16 infra. And, the options at the end of the term set forth in Section 17 infra., Fair Market Value will be determined by agreement of the parties. If unable to agree, then a licensed Real Estate Appraiser will determine Fair Market Value. The cost of the appraisal will be shared equally by both parties. If the parties are unable to agree upon an appraiser, then each party may, at their own expense, select an appraiser. The two appraisers so selected shall either determine the value of the PROPERTY, or if they are unable to do so, they shall select a third appraiser, the cost of which will be borne by both parties, and the third appraiser, will make the final determination of the Fair Market Value.

16. RIGHT OF REFUSAL: OWNER/INVESTOR and OWNER/OCCUPANT shall each have a right of first refusal regarding the PROPERTY. Should either party during the term of this Agreement elect to sell their interest in the PROPERTY, that party must give written notice of that fact, and provide a copy of the written offer to purchase to the non-selling party. The non-selling party

7

Sample Document

EQUITY SHARE CO-TENANCY AGREEMENT OF JOINT OWNERSHIP (8 OF 11 PAGES)

shall have ten (10) days from receipt of said written notice within which to respond upon the same Terms and Conditions to the written notice to sell.

    A. Should the non-selling party elect to buy the selling party's interest, they shall have thirty (30) days from the date of giving the selling party a written notice of their intent to buy the selling party's interest in the PROPERTY within which to secure financing. Escrow used to purchase the other Equity Share partner's interest, not to exceed sixty (60) days from the written offer and acceptance.

    B. Should the non-selling party be unable to secure the required financing necessary to buy selling party's interest, they may then accept the purchaser of the selling party's interest as a new Co-Owner to the same Terms and Conditions as the original Joint Ownership Agreement, or sell their interest in the Property, in conjunction with the other Co-Owner.

17. **OPTIONS AT END OF TERM:** There are several options for dissolution of the Joint Ownership Agreement, either at end of term, or, if the parties so choose, prior to end of term. Buyout terms, which are different than those set down in this section, will require mutual written agreement between OWNER/OCCUPANT and OWNER/INVESTOR. Unless otherwise specified, the buyout shall be based on Fair Market Value, as defined in Section 15 of this Agreement. The OWNER/OCCUPANT will have the first right to buy out the OWNER/INVESTOR, under subsections A, B, or C. The OWNER/OCCUPANT must state their intentions, in writing, to the OWNER/INVESTOR, at least ninety (90) days before the expiration date of this Agreement.

    A. OWNER/OCCUPANT acquires cash from a separate source and buys out the OWNER/INVESTOR without refinancing the PROPERTY. Distribution of equity per Section 18 of this Agreement.

    B. OWNER/OCCUPANT gets a new loan and buys out OWNER/INVESTOR. OWNER/INVESTOR agrees to cooperate with lender and the title company to facilitate refinancing. Distribution of equity, is as per Section 18 of this Agreement.

    C. OWNER/OCCUPANT assigns their rights in this Agreement, including OWNER/OCCUPANT'S buyout rights, to a third party, who then buys out the OWNER/INVESTOR, using the methods described in subsections A or B above. Distribution of equity, is as per Section 18 of this Agreement. An assignment by OWNER/OCCUPANT, under this subsection (i.e., subsection C), may only occur at the end of the 36-month term of this Equity Share Agreement, or any extensions of the term, mutually agreed to by OWNER/OCCUPANT and OWNER/INVESTOR, in writing, and shall not be subject to any limitations on assignments set forth in Section 10 of this Agreement, and shall not be subject to the

8

Sample Document

EQUITY SHARE CO-TENANCY AGREEMENT OF JOINT OWNERSHIP (9 OF 11 PAGES)

OWNER/INVESTORS' right of first refusal, set forth in Section 16 of this Agreement.

D. OWNER/INVESTOR buys out OWNER/OCCUPANT. Distribution of equity is as per Section 18 of this Agreement.

E. If neither the OWNER/OCCUPANT nor the OWNER/INVESTOR elect to buy out the other, then the OWNER/OCCUPANT and the OWNER/INVESTOR shall jointly sell their ownership interests in the PROPERTY to a third party. OWNER/OCCUPANT agrees to maintain the property in good condition, permit lock-key access to the brokerage agreed upon by both parties, permits open houses, and, in general, acts in good faith for showing, selling, and closing to a third party. Distribution of equity as per paragraph 18.

18. DISTRIBUTION OF PROCEEDS:

A. OWNER/OCCUPANT will be responsible for 100% of the real estate commission and non-recurring closing costs if property is sold.

B. If the PROPERTY is to be sold, costs of preparation for sale will be deducted before any division of profit. Preparation of the sale does not include termite work, roof repair, or costs because of non-maintenance.

C. OWNER/INVESTOR to receive an amount equal to their initial contribution, as set forth in Section 3. Initial contribution by OWNER/INVESTOR is $0.00.

D. OWNERS/INVESTOR to receive any additional contributions made towards capital improvements, or advances on the First Deed of Trust.

E. OWNER/OCCUPANT shall receive an amount equal to their initial contribution, which is zero.

F. OWNER/OCCUPANT shall receive amount credited for capital improvements, under Sections 8 and 9 of this Agreement.

G. Any principal reduction in the Deed of Trust, and not used to acquire the PROPERTY, will be credited to the OWNER/OCCUPANT. Any negative interest added to the original loan balance will be the obligation of the OWNER/OCCUPANT.

H. The remaining proceeds shall be divided between the parties based on their percentages of ownership in the property which is 0% to the OWNER/INVESTORS and 0% to OWNER/OCCUPANT. The OWNER/INVESTORS have the right to either choose their percentage of the upside equity split or a 12% yearly return on their initial investment.

9

Sample Document

EQUITY SHARE CO-TENANCY AGREEMENT OF JOINT OWNERSHIP (10 OF 11 PAGES)

19. TRANSFER FREE OF LEINS: In the event of any sale, the selling party shall furnish to the purchasing party marketable title, free of liens and judgments, as evidenced by a policy of title insurance.

20. INDEMNITY: OWNER/OCCUPANT and OWNER/INVESTOR, agree to hold harmless, and indemnify and defend, the other party's interest in the PROPERTY, against any and all mechanics liens, any involuntary liens, claims, actions, losses, damages, and costs and expenses, including attorney's fees, whether for injury or damage to persons or property, or otherwise, arising from any act or omission of any person, occurring on or about the PROPERTY, or from the occupancy, or use of the property by either party, or either party's employees, agents, or invitees.

21. OWNER/OCCUPANT'S OBLIGATION TO REIMBURSE OWNER/INVESTOR FOR ADVANCES: Upon closing, OWNER/OCCUPANT will be responsible for making all mortgage loan payments, as well as property tax and insurance payments on the PROPERTY, as required in Section 4.A. of this Agreement. If OWNER/OCCUPANT fails to make any such payments within ten (10) days from it being due, then the OWNER/INVESTOR may cure the default by advancing the payment to the party to whom it is owed. The OWNER/OCCUPANT shall be immediately pay to the OWNER/INVESTOR the amount so advance. Failure to make this payment shall be deemed a default, within the meaning of Section 11.A. of this Agreement.

22. WRITE-OFFS: Both parties are to seek advice of a CPA to determine tax benefits.

23. FAILURE OF OWNER/OCCUPANT TO ACHIEVE FINANCING: If the OWNER/OCCUPANT desires to buy out OWNER/INVESTOR, but cannot get financing, then the OWNER/INVESTOR has the option to extend the terms of this Agreement, sell to the OWNER/OCCUPANT on terms, or find another OWNER/INVESTOR(S) that might be wiling to buy out the existing OWNER/INVESTOR.

24. HEIRS, ASSIGNS AND SUCCESSORS: This Agreement is binding upon and insures to the benefit of the heirs, assigns and successors in interest of the parties. All heirs and successors are bound by the same Terms and Condition as the original parties to this Agreement.

25. RENTAL AGREEMENT: OWNER/OCCUPANT will sign a Rental Agreement with OWNER/INVESTOR, to cover Fair Rent on the OWNER/INVESTOR'S 0% ownership interest on the PROPERTY. OWNER/OCCUPANT will pay all of the loan and property tax payments, and in return, will receive a credit for the Fair Rent that would have been paid to the OWNER/INVESTOR. The rental will be used only if OWNER/INVESTOR

10

Sample Document

EQUITY SHARE CO-TENANCY AGREEMENT OF JOINT OWNERSHIP (11 OF 11 PAGES)

desires to be active in treating the PROPRTY as a rental. Fair Rent will be at $ 0.00 a month, to be used as a credit.

26. **EXCLUSIVE RIGHTS:** The OWNER/OCCUPANT shall have exclusive rights to occupancy and possession of the PROPRTY. The OWNER/INVESTOR shall have no rights to occupancy or visitation without permission from the OWNER/OCCUPANT.

27. **Severability:** The provisions of this Agreement, and the invalidity of any portion, shall not invalidate the remainder.

28. **ATTORNEY FEES:** In any action or proceeding involving a dispute between OWNER/INVESTOR and OWNER/OCCUPANT arising out of this Agreement, the Addendum, the Purchase Agreement, the Deed of Trust, the person(s) prevailing will be entitled to recover reasonable Attorney Fees and any costs incurred from the non-prevailing party.

29. **DISCLOSURE BY EQUITY SHARE GROUP AND (NAME):**
This Agreement is prepared per the instructions of OWNER/OCCUPANT and OWNER/INVESTOR. Equity Share Group and (Name) advises both parties to seek the advice of both a Real Estate Attorney and a Tax Attorney, or Accountant, as to the validity of the documentation and this transaction. Equity Share Group and (Name) do not guarantee property values, or the capability of either party to perform their contractual obligations. Equity Share Group and (Name) make no representations, whether oral or written, as to future Real Property values, possible appreciation, or Real Estate market conditions or prospects, in general. Each party acknowledges that he/she has received no such representations from either Equity Share Group, (Name), or any of their employees, agents, or representatives. It is the responsibility of the OWNER/OCCUPANT and OWNER/INVESTOR to get title insurance, escrow closing, disclosure and legal advice, perform due diligence, investigate market conditions, and to comply with all legal and contractual provisions. Existing financing might contain a Due-on-Sale clause.

IN WITNESS WHEREOF the parties have executed this Agreement as set forth below.

Dated: _____   Name: _____
                                           OWNER/OCCUPANT

Dated: _____   Name: _____
                                           OWNER/INVESTOR

Sample Document

3. ADDENDUM FAIR RENTAL AGREEMENT TO THE JOINT OWNERSHIP AGREEMENT

ADDENDUM
FAIR RENTAL AGREEMENT
TO THE JOINT OWNERSHIP AGREEMENT

RECEIVED FROM   (Name)   ,   (vesting)   , herein referred to as the Tenant, the sum of $ 000,000.00, (Some Hundred Dollars). Evidenced by (no deposit necessary). Upon acceptance of this Agreement, the Owner of the premises, will apply the deposit as follows:

Rent for the period from   (Date)   until   (Date)   with a credit of $ 0,000.00 a year.
Other: This Rental Agreement will be renewed yearly through _____ , as long as the Joint Ownership Agreement stays in affect.
        Tenant offers to rent from the Owner interest in the premises situated in the City of _____ ,
County of _____, State of California
Described : (Address), City, CA
Upon the following Terms and Conditions:
1. TERMS: The terms will commence on   (Date)   , and continue until   (Date)   , for a total rent of $ _____ credit per year.
2. RENT: Rent will be $ _____ per month, (the payment of rent can be in the form of a credit of the mortgage payment and related costs.
3. MULTIPLE OCCUPANCY: See the Joint Ownership Agreement as to other occupancy of premises other that the Owner/Occupant.
4. UTILITIES: Tenant will be responsible for the payment of all utilities and services.
5. USE: The premises will be used exclusively as a residence for no more than four persons.
6. ORDINANCES AND STATUTES: Tenant will comply with all statutes, ordinances and requirements of all municipal, state and federal authorities now in force, or which may later be in force, regarding the use of the premises.
7. ASSIGNMENT AND SUBLETTING: Tenant will not assign this Agreement or sublet any portion of the premises without prior written consent of the Owner.
8. MAINTENANCE AND REPAIRS: See Joint Ownership Agreement
9. INVENTORY: Personal Property that was a part of the purchase (e.g., Stove, dishwasher) will be maintained by Tenant.
10. DAMAGES TO PREMISES: Per the Joint Ownership Agreement, the insurance will cover all damages, with the Tenant paying the deductible and maintaining the premises in an as is condition as to the time of purchase.
11. ENTRY AND INSPECTION: Owner will have the right to enter the premises (a) in case of emergency, (b) if property is abandoned for more than sixty (60) days.
12. INDEMNIFICATION: Owner will not be liable for any damage or injury to Tenant, or any other person, or to any property, occurring on the premises.
13. DEFAULT: The Terms and Conditions of the Joint Ownership Agreement, if the items agreed to on this Agreement are violated, then this Fair Rental Agreement will also be voided.
14. TIME: Time is of the essence of this Agreement.
15. ATTORNEY FEES: In any action or proceedings involving a dispute between Owner and Tenant, arising out of this Fair Rental Agreement, the person prevailing will be entitled to reasonable attorney fees and any costs incurred.
16. CONDITIONS: The terms of this Rental Agreement are the same as the conditions of the existing Equity Share Agreement between Owner/Investor and Owner/Occupant. The purpose of the Agreement is for the Owner/Occupant to rent the Owner/Investor's share of the home.
17. ENTIRE AGREEMENT: The forgoing constitutes the entire Agreement. The existing Joint Ownership Agreement between the parties will define the terms of this Rental contract.

Tenant _____ Dated: _____   Owner_____ Dated: _____
        (Name)   (Name)

Tenant _____ Dated: _____   Owner _____ Dated: _____
        (Name)   (Name)

Sample Document

CHAPTER SIX

THE LEASE OPTION CONVERSION PROGRAM

Real estate is one of the best investments people can make. It is also one of the largest investments in a person's life. To the potential buyer, "home-ownership" means:

- Security

- Equity build-up

- Tax benefits

- Pride of ownership

The average person, who is tired of renting and wants to start the process of "home ownership," needs to look at ways to accomplish his/her goal. The real estate market has always had creative programs such as lease option/rent-to-own along with other conditional purchases. And lease option/rent-to-own idea is becoming more familiar to the general public as an alternative way to purchase real estate. The main problem with these types of purchases has always been two-fold:

1. Finding parties to participate who are also well-educated about these types of programs.

2. Having a buyer who will be able to assume ownership of the home and property.

The buyer, potential homeowner/occupant, wants a place to live, tax benefits, and the opportunity to build equity in his/her investment. The most common reasons preventing a Buyer from achieving ownership of his/her own home are:

- Lack of down payment

- Sub-par credit

- Desired location
- Time restrictions

The investor is also looking for an investment that will allow the following:

- Minimum down payment (20% down is usually required)
- No loans
- No negative cash-flow
- Location
- Write-offs
- Tax benefits
- 1031 Tax Exchange potential

Equity Share Group has been putting creative programs together for home buyers and investors since 1980, and has participated in hundreds of transactions ranging from conventional purchases, exchanges, lease options and equity shares for buyers and investors who have all accomplished "home-ownership" and/or investment profit.

The Equity Share Group programs have helped hundreds of home buyers and investors accomplish their real estate goals. The equity share program is the practice of putting two parties together—home buyer and investor—as tenants-in-common so that each party can profit from his/her ownership interest.

The Equity Share Group has also developed a new program that will help the serious home buyer make his/her dream of "home ownership" come true. The new lease option conversion program (LOC Program) combines the equity share program with a lease option program that work very well together.

HOW THE LEASE OPTION CONVERSION PROGRAM (LOC PROGRAM) WORKS

The lease option conversion program is a conditional sale of real estate with the commitment from the lessee/buyer to meet certain contractual terms such as sales price, option time period and other specified conditions before the sale is completed. All parties must agree that the property in question is being sold under terms and not for cash. The lessee/buyer is basically renting the property from the lessor/seller with a commitment to purchase the property within the agreed upon timeframe.

During the lease option time period, the Internal Revenue Service will not recognize the lease option as a sale, since no property has changed ownership. The lessee/buyer does not receive tax benefits under the lease option program, and the lessor/seller receives normal investor benefits.

Most real estate professionals do not get involved with any types of creative transactions. The parties involved need to be aware that lease options require dealing with clients for a minimum of one year, while they execute the terms and conditions necessary to complete the contract. Most lease options take two or more years.

The liability factor becomes greater when there is a conditional sale. Over the past ten years, attempting more than one hundred lease options where the lessee/buyer is able to execute the contract and obtain total ownership the in-full-completion success ratio has only been about 30%. The primary reason for non-performance is attributed to the lessee/buyer not being able to save up enough down payment money to qualify for an offset loan.

The lease option conversion program raises this success ratio because it combines the lease option with the equity share program making the success ratio approximately 70% versus the usual 30%.

WHY THE LEASE OPTION CONVERSION PROGRAM WORKS

The key to investing is to maximize the benefits and minimize the risks. The three main areas our LOC Program covers, that an ordinary lease option does not are:

1. The LOC Program is structured to allow the lessee/buyer to earn enough credits for a down payment. However, in order to exercise the home purchase option the lessee/buyer is required to have good credit, a favorable loan, and terms that will make the execution successful. A lessee/buyer with bad credit will have to enter a credit repair program.

2. The LOC Program establishes a timetable that will benefit both the lessor/seller and lessee/buyer to maximize his/her investment potential.

3. Finally, our LOC Program can be structured so that both parties enjoy the benefits. The lessor/seller can setup a payment plan similar to a triple-net lease (NNN) that will show no negative cash-flow and positive equity build-up.

The ideal client for the LOC Program is a lessee/buyer who needs some time and wants to live in a specific location but lacks down payment money.

Equity Share Group has processed over five hundred LOC Program transactions during the past fifteen years. In all cases, the full contract has been executed, and the specific rules and regulations that meet the Internal Revenue criteria have been followed. Approximately 70% of all new clients the Equity Share Group interviews are able to complete the LOC Program process and become homeowners.

The lease option conversion plan almost guarantees the lessee/buyer "home ownership" and the investor can maintain his/her investment with no property management problems. The return factor for both parties is very good. The time period for a lease option contract will depend on the economy.

NORMAL INVESTOR PURCHASE
Conventional Home Purchase

Purchase Price	$ 400,000

Home Buyer

Property purchased in buyer's own name requires a minimum of 20% down (Investors who want to own need a minimum of 20% to 35% down to show a break-even cash-flow)	$ 80,000
Adjustable Loan with one-year prepay penalty	$ 320,000
Fair Rent	$ 1,600/month

Loan payment, taxes, insurance, etc.	$ 2,100/month

Negative cash-flow with a normal rental is $ 500/month
(plus repairs, taxes, and insurance)

Negative is more like $ 900/month
Property appreciation will range from 1% to
3% per year, over the next three years

Equity Share Program Purchase
With the equity share program the buyer is only required to put
3% to 10% down to own.

Purchase Price	$ 400,000
Investor contribution (5%)	$ 20,000
Buyer/occupant contribution (5%)	$ 20,000

Ownership is tenants-in-common
as to a 60% buyer/40% investor split

Buyer/occupant gets financing

First deed of trust (90%)	$ 360,000
Down payment (5% buyer/5% investor)	$ 40,000

Term – five to seven years

Buyer/occupant – pays principal, interest, taxes and insurance (upkeep)

Buyer/occupant write-offs – interest and property taxes

Investor write-offs – depreciation, repairs, insurance, HOA Fees

Buyout – based on fee appraisal

Buyout
Appraised value	$ 450,000

Buyer/occupant usually refinances and purchases
the investors' interest in the property

Investor usually does a 1031 Tax Exchange with buyout

Investor – original investment		$ 20,000
Split of upside equity – new value		$ 450,000
Original value	$400,000 =	$ 50,000
Investor receives original investment		$ 20,000
Plus upside of		$ 20,000
Investor – total received on investment		$ 40,000
Buyer/occupant receives 100% ownership with original investment		$ 20,000 Plus
		$ 30,000 Equity

Approximate Total   **$ 50,000**

Other program stipulations are:

- This program requires buyer/occupant to have fairly good credit and the potential for a buyout
- The buyer/occupant can also sell the property after the contract time period, but must pay all costs of sale
- *Under the current market conditions, five years should be an adequate time period for the market to move upwards.*

Lease Option Program (LOC Program) Example

The lease option conversion program can combine a lease option with an equity share if needed.

Lessor – Seller/Owner	
Lessee – Buyer/Occupant	
Value Determined at signing of Option Agreement	$400,000
Normal Rent	$ 1,600/month

Term – two years, or longer

Option Money (towards purchase)	$ 10,000

Monthly payments/Triple-Net (NNN) $ 2,100/month
(NNN represents – interest payment on loan,
pro-rated property taxes, and pro-rated insurance)

Exercising Option – Credit for Option Money, percentage of monthly payment, or percentage of property appreciation

Lessee/Buyer will enter into a Lease Option Conversion for a two-year time period (given the present state of the economy, the time period might take longer)

Lessee/Buyer will pay the full $ 2,100/month
plus an initial deposit of $ 10,000

Lessee/Buyer will pay upkeep $ 2,100/month
plus a portion of expenses (Similar to Triple-Net Lease (NNN) – Interest payment on loan, pro-rated property taxes, and pro-rated insurance)

2-Year Appraisal shows value at $ 436,000

Lessee/Buyer needs to qualify for a 90% loan
(Possible FHA – 97% Loan)

90% Loan – Based on a sales price of $ 436,000

Loan amount will be $ 392,400

Lessee/Buyer Down Payment (10%) $ 43,600

Lessee/Buyer (Lease Option) credits
$10,000 plus 50% of upside ($36,000) $ 28,000

Lessor/Seller Equity $ 15,600

Equity Share split for three to five years –
Buyer 55%/Investor 45%
Investor has no loans in his/her name

Investor's original $20,000 equity can be transferred through a 1031 Tax Exchange to another property

Investor's remaining equity of approximately $18,000 stays in the property, as a "Joint Ownership," if the property is deferred

Investor – Keeps a 40% ownership in the existing property.

Buyer – Keeps 60% ownership in the property, with all of the tax benefits.

The Equity Share Group LOC Program provides a way for renters to have the opportunity to purchase a home. In addition, investors are able to purchase a property in a good location without negative cash-flow or management problems, and will have a built-in buyer for the future. In the end, both parties have a great investment with little or no risk.

AN EXAMPLE OF HOW A "LEASE OPTION CONVERSION" WORKS

The "Lease Option Conversion Program" only works if all parties work together and allow enough time for property values to appreciate. The lessee (potential owner) not only needs to live up to the terms and conditions of the contract but must have the ability to exercise the contract.

In 2004, the Equity Share Group put a couple into a home in Elk Grove, California with the idea that by 2006, they would have saved up enough credits to be able to exercise the option they agreed to. The couple put up $5,000 as "option money," paid $2,200 a month, and they maintained the home. In 2004, a home like theirs was renting for about $1,700 a month in that area.

The seller/lessors of the home also agreed that if the buyer/lessees lived up to all of the terms, they would make up the difference for the 10% down, upon exercising the option. The value of the home agreed upon by all parties was $300,000. In 2006, the buyer/lessees were ready to exercise their right to purchase. The Lender acknowledged that the credits for the initial $5,000, plus a $500 a month credit for twenty-four months, amounted to a total of $17,000 in credits from buyer/Lessees, and the total down payment needed for the 10% was $30,000. The seller/lessors agreed to add in the remaining $13,000 at close, as a "hybrid" joint ownership. The buyer/lessees closed the transaction, still own the home, bought out the seller/lessors, and now have all of the benefits of home ownership. Because of the loan rates at the time the new owners exercised their option, they have a payment almost equal to their lease option payment of $2,200—and, their tax benefits give them a write-off of about $28,000 a year between interest and property taxes.

My "Lease Option Conversion Program" could not only turn you from a renter into being a property owner but would also give you the added benefit of saving up the down payment while you live in the home.

Over the past twenty years this program has helped many couples achieve home ownership but it only works if you understand exactly what you want, do not get in over your head — and finally, have the flexibility to be able to extend the time periods necessary to accomplish your goals.

Lease options don't always work out though. If a "lessee" (buyer) enters into a contract and agrees to pay more than the normal rent with the added "option payment" they have to understand that if over the term of the agreement they cannot perform, then it will become apparent that, at some point unless all parties can come to an agreement the lessee/buyer will lose his/her right to purchase the property.

If you combine a "lease option" with the "joint ownership program" and all parties agree to the terms and the extended time period, then the control benefits to all participants will be a successful outcome.

I have had buyer/lessees who wanted to enter into a lease option purchase subject to eventually getting a loan, coming up with the down payment, and making sure all of the terms to the agreement were met. Then, due to job status, credit problems, not being able to save the down payment money, and/or other miscellaneous issues they could not exercise the option and lost their right to purchase the home.

Always negotiate a contract that has extensions and make sure you analyze any contract you enter into so that unforeseen problems that might come up can be handled and negotiated.

FREQUENTLY ASKED QUESTIONS

What is a real estate investment?

An investment in real estate takes two forms:

1. **Home ownership** – An investment in real estate that is your permanent residence is very important for a number of reasons. First, you get to live in your investment while it's working for you. The tax benefits alone make it worth the effort to try to own a home. Your investment of owning a home to live in brings wealth in the following ways: interest deduction, equity build-up, mortgage reduction and appreciation in the overall economy in which you reside.

2. **Investment property** – The ownership of investment property is different than owning a permanent residence. Most wealthy people in this country started with real estate. Investors look at real estate differently than they do a permanent residence because they are not living on the property but want to have the tax and investment advantages.

What is a lease option?

The basic lease option is a conditional sale, where the buyer/lessee and seller/lessor agree to terms and conditions today for a final result to take place at a later date. Basically, a lease option is a contingent sale with certain terms that must be carried out in the future. The seller/lessor must be able to provide good title to the property and the buyer/lessee must be able to get a loan or be able to purchase the property as agreed upon in the contract.

Who are the parties in a lease option?

The seller on the contract is called the seller/lessor and the buyer is called the buyer/lessee. The lease option does not convey title at the time of its execution. It sets up a contract outlining the terms, and at some point, the buyer/lessee must finalize the contract.

When a lease/option is agreed upon by all parties how can both the seller/lessor and buyer/lessee be protected and have his/her option acknowledged?

It is mandatory that when you execute a lease option that a "MEMORANDUM OF LEASE OPTION" be recorded in the county where the property is located. The recording of this document is important for the buyer/lessee because it clouds the title of the seller/lessor's property and makes the public aware that you have a written agreement to purchase this property at a later date. By having the memorandum recorded, the lessor/seller can no longer borrow against or sell the property to someone else. Recording the memorandum protects the seller/lessor, because it prevents the buyer/lessee from claiming that he/she did not understand that the option was a potential purchase and not a rental.

What should the real estate agent representing the buyer/lessee make sure the contract contains?

It is the responsibility of the real estate agent and the buyer/lessee when they enter into a lease option agreement, to make sure that the following steps take place during the transaction:

- All lease options should have an escrow opened during the option period so that all option money, reports and necessary documentation can be kept. Also the lender working with the buyer/lessee needs to work with the escrow company while they are pre-approving their client.

- A memorandum must be recorded in the county where the property is located.

- The following reports should be carefully reviewed and addressed before the lease option is executed: roof, termite, home warranty, disclosures, and preliminary report must all be acknowledged and accepted prior to the buyer/lessee moving into the property.

- It is important that the seller/lessor must show the ability to convey good title to the property once the option is exercised.

The preliminary report from the title company will show who owns the property, what liens are against the property and if there any defects that must be removed prior to the option being exercised.

- The "option" date must be acknowledged by all parties and it should be understood that neither the seller/lessor, the listing realtor, nor the selling realtor can guarantee the lessee's ability to exercise the option at the end of the option period.

- The lessee must be aware that should the lease option not be exercised, due to non-performance of the potential buyer, the lease option agreement will be terminated and the property will convert back to the seller/lessor. The lessee will not recover any of his/her option money or monthly credit paid during the lease period. If the lessee does not exercise his/her option then the property will be vacated and converted back to the seller/lessor.

What makes up a lease option agreement?

The contents of the lease option are important because they make up the items that have been agreed upon for future consideration. The terms addressed are:

- Name of buyer/lessee
- Option money
- Sales price
- Property description
- Monthly payments
- Credit towards purchase
- Option date agreed upon
- Extensions if any
- Repair and maintenance
- Tax benefits
- Insurance

- Default or arbitration
- Buyout terms
- Recording Memorandum
- Disclosures
- Approved reports (roof, termite, property, preliminary)
- Escrow procedures
- Expenses to close at the end of the agreement
- Home warranty
- Commission

Is the lease option agreement signed by all parties and considered a binding contract?

A signed and agreed upon lease option that has been delivered and contracted is a binding agreement. The only difference is that a lease option is a conditional sale, usually based on certain contingencies (conditions) being exercised or completed. If the buyer/lessee or the seller/lessor fails to live up to the agreed upon contract then the valid agreement can become void due to non-execution.

What happens if the property value goes up or down at the time the lease option is exercised?

The lease option is a binding contract; the sales price agreed upon at the time the contract is signed is the price at which the property will be purchased.

What qualifications does a buyer/lessee need to have?

It depends on the requirements of the seller/lessor, as to what the conditions of qualification will be for the purchase of a property under the lease option program. The general terms and conditions are usually favorable to the buyer/lessee.

Through the Lease Option Conversion Program how does the buyer/lessee build up the potential down payment money?

The "option money" credits and/or the upside appreciation (equity growth).

What if there is no equity growth over a 2-year Lease Option?

There are alternative ways to making the lease option work:

a. Extend the time period

b. Instead of the equity growth, the seller/lessor can give the buyer/lessee a credit for the difference between what rent would have been and the lease payment (NNN) made (e.g., rent is $1600/month, and lease option payment is $2100/month, the difference would be $500 x 24 months = $12,000. This amount would be the credit towards the down payment).

c. Seller/lessor an add more money to the buyer/lessee's down payment and convert the lease option to a straight equity share. The lessee/buyer will take out a new loan removing the seller/lessor's name from the old loan.

What will the buyer/lessee need, to qualify, when it comes time to exercise the "option?"

The buyer/lessee will need the following:

• A down payment (done through credits)

• Good credit

• Property to appraise

• Seller/lessor's participation

If the buyer/lessee qualifies on his/her own will he/she need the seller/lessor's participation?

No. The buyer/lessee can exercise the "option" on his/her own and will still get the credited money but the seller/lessor will not leave money in the property.

CHAPTER SEVEN

THE CONCEPT OF CONTRACT OF SALE

Thirty years ago the "contract of sale" was used to facilitate real estate transactions. In the old days this type of deal was delegated to the sale of land with $100 dollars down and financing of the remaining balance over a time period agreed upon by all parties.

With the contract of sale sellers and buyers in a down-turned economy seek ways to either sell or purchase property in the most creative ways possible.

Unlike conventional means the contract of sale allows the seller (vendor) to create financing with the benefit of getting a better purchase price — a better return, and a much easier way to market his/her property.

The buyer who doesn't have 10 – 20% down payment, excellent credit, or the capability to close on real estate today can still enter the market with the current discounted values. The benefit to the buyer (vendee) is tremendous. Buyers with good income can purchase today with all the tax benefits of "home ownership." Buyers can have time to rebuild their credit and save up necessary money and have time to adjust to the market or "home ownership."

The decision of whether to do a "lease option" or a "contract of sale" must be looked at based on what the benefits are. Remember most people who have a good income but have poor credit or are unable to get financing can be helped. The "contract of sale conversion program" offers buyers the benefit of owning property under terms and conditions with tax benefits.

In 2007, I owned a home in California that I was renting for $3,000 a month that was good but did not cover the mortgage payment, taxes, HOA fees, and the maintenance. For the first year I had a negative monthly output of $1,300 continuing into the second year. Towards the end of 2007, I did a contract of sale on the property for a value of $940,000, approximately $50,000 over today's value. The new buyer/vendee agreed to pay $3,800 a month plus all of the insurance, HOA fees, property taxes, and everyday expenses.

I will be paid off in 2010, my monthly negative has been taken care off, and the initial down payment was $35,000. I have just gone from possibly losing this property due to negative cash-flow to being able to get my equity out of the property over time.

If I do get paid off in 2010, I will receive the rest of my equity and be able to move my investment forward. The buyer/occupants will have purchased this property, gotten all of the tax benefits, and can continue living in a home that will meet their needs in the future. The contract of sale is an avenue for people who have ruined their credit or do not have the down payment to be able to purchase a home in today's market.

Owner/investors that had to take back properties due to delinquency need to either get rid of their investments or at least reduce the monthly negative cash-flow so that they can profit.

If the buyer/vendee does not pay off the obligation then through the legal process they will lose their investment or be penalized. The contract of sale will allow both parties to either purchase-on-terms or minimize the negative of owning real estate in today's market.

The basic concept of a contract of sale is to create seller financing and allow a buyer to get into the housing market.

In 2006, a friend of mine purchased a property in San Ramon, California as an investment. At the time the $730,000 purchase price was at least $50,000 under value and the seller, who had just lost her husband, was willing to do a rent-back for $2,500 a month. But to cover the mortgage, HOA fees, and property taxes, the monthly payment amounted to about $2,900, a negative of approximately $400 a month.

In 2007, because of the negative cash-flow, my friend decided to contract the property out for a three-year time period. The down payment was $10,000, and the buyer/vendee agreed to pay $3,500 a month, plus property taxes, HOA fees, and miscellaneous charges connected with the property.

The benefit of the contract of sale is that the seller/vendor can stop the negative cash-flow and the buyer/vendee can purchase a property with terms. In 2011, my friend will receive the rest of his equity and be able to at least advance his real estate investment.

The buyer/vendee upon improving his credit will have enough credits towards purchase. This is a win-win situation.

Not all contracts of sale work but if the buyer/vendee lives up to all of the terms and conditions then everything can work. If the buyer/vendee defaults, due to job status, then the seller/vendor has no alternative but to take action to get the property back.

When you enter into a contract of sale all parties must be aware of the economy and its ups and downs. If over a three to five year period there is no growth and interest rates do not support a new loan, then all parties must agree up front to extend the terms of the original agreement. Any contract that has strict time restrictions or term limits usually indicates the possibility of something going wrong.

As a professional over the years it has been obvious to me that we have no control over interest rates, appreciation, and other variables that might affect real estate. There must always be an exit plan to any term contract. The questions that must be acknowledged and understood are as follows:

What is a "contract of sale"?

A contract of sale is the conveyance of equitable title in a property. Equitable title is ownership that allows you to benefit in the process of tax advantages, equity build up and rights of possession. A contract of sale does not give you fee title or complete rights.

Who are the parties to a contract of sale?

The owner (fee) is called the "vendor" and the purchaser/buyer, the "vendee," is the equitable owner. Title does not pass to the buyer/vendee and there are no rights to borrow on or sell the property without the consent of the owner/vendor.

What type of ownership is conveyed with the contract of sale?

Ownership is an "equitable title" giving an interest of ownership but not "fee title."

With an "equitable title" arrangement what benefits does the buyer/vendee receive?

The buyer/vendee receives the benefit of tax write-offs such as interest and property taxes for a primary residence and multi write-offs for an investor.

How does a "creative approach" like a contract of sale help a potential buyer get into the real estate market?

Usually a contract of sale requires a smaller down payment, between 5% and 8%, and any existing loans on the property are taken "subject to." The potential buyer/vendee does not need perfect credit and has time to work towards saving more money for the final payoff, less the down payment, tax benefits, time to repair credit and, finally, purchasing at today's lower market values.

Does the Internal Revenue Service (IRS) recognize the contract of sale?

The IRS will treat the purchase of property under a contract of sale as an equitable interest in the subject property. Unlike a lease option the buyer/vendee will be able to write-off interest, property taxes and other items if they are treating the purchase as an investment.

What makes up the terms and conditions of a contract of sale?

The contract of sale is made up of the following items:

- Purchase price
- Monthly payments
- Property taxes and insurance
- Supporting documents
- Exit plan for new loan or sale of property
- Maintenance
- Assignment of contract

Upon the buyer/vendee purchasing the property with the contract of sale are there any documents recorded to protect the new buyer/vendee?

The title company will record a document called a memorandum of contract of sale. This document encumbers the property showing in public records that a contract exists between both parties and that equitable ownership has passed hands. The title company will issue title insurance protecting all parties and guaranteeing good title for buyout or future sale.

What is the marketing approach to the contract of sale?

Anytime you become creative with real estate the marketing approach becomes easier. People who make a great income but have damaged credit are very interested because they can purchase with terms, get tax benefits, and wait for a bad economy to recover.

How can the purchaser/vendee profit by using the contract of sale when purchasing real estate?

The profit comes in the form of being able to purchase a property with terms, get the benefits, and eventually sell the investment when the market recovers. Profit in real estate is always determined by return and benefit.

How does the buyer/vendee exercise the contract of sale at the end of the time period?

At the end of the contract period or when all parties agree the buyer/vendee will go to a lender, produce the documentation of ownership and if there is enough equity, they will refinance and buyout the seller/vendor. If, at the time of the buyout, there is not enough equity then the seller/vendor can allow a conversion by doing a partial buyout, deed over the property to the buyer/vendee, and then create a second deed of trust for the difference.

Can you combine a purchase with a contract of sale and an equity share investor?

Yes. The hybrid you can create would be that the seller/vendor sells to the buyer/vendee on a contract of sale. The seller/vendor's equity in the property can stay there until the buyer/vendee wants to buyout the seller/vendor. If for financing reasons or for a better return to the seller/vendor it would be possible to create a sale with the seller/vendor carrying back a percentage of ownership in the property for future return.

If the property being purchased has an existing loan encumbering it is that loan taken subject to by the buyer/vendee?

Yes. It is necessary for the protection of the seller/vendor's credit that you set up a collection account that has the buyer/vendee pay a third party. The money is then disbursed to the existing lender and the remaining funds to the seller/vendor.

How does the seller/vendor protect his/her credit and make sure that the existing loan on the property is being paid on a monthly basis?

The seller/vendor must control the payment to his/her mortgage either through a collection company or by having the vendee/buyer pay him/her directly, and then he/she forwards the exiting mortgage payment to his/her lender. As proof all payments must be given to both seller/vendor and buyer/vendee.

To execute a contract of sale how does a new lender analyze a buyer who has had this type of ownership for refinancing?

The new lender will see through the preliminary report they order for the refinance or sale and that a memorandum of contract has been recorded. The fee title will appear in the seller/vendor's name but the report will show that the buyer/vendee has equitable title. The sender will also see that upon the seller/vendor's demand in escrow of payoff, that a grant deed is already signed and notarized to give fee title to the buyer/vendee.

How can the seller/vendor profit by selling his/her property using a contract of sale?

Any time you are creative and allow the buyer to get into a property with terms you have created a win-win situation. The type of buyer you will attract is someone who needs help with a full down payment, needs help with his/her credit, or needs time to sell an existing property, in order to have a regular sale to take place. To a lot of buyers, a lease option (no write-offs) will not serve the same purpose as a contract of sale.

If there is an existing deed of trust on a subject property with a "due on sale" clause can it be "called?"

Yes. A "due on sale" can be called by a transfer of title, without the lender's consent — but more likely due to the fee title not transferring the lender will not exercise the calling of the loan option.

How does the contract of sale concept affect the real estate broker/agent during the course of the transaction?

The real estate broker/agent can show the seller how, in a bad real estate market, it will still be possible to attract potential buyers. If the seller must relocate or needs to sell due to financial reasons, a house sitting on the market for six months is going to create a hardship. Renting the house will probably create a negative cash flow. Finally, with the contract of sale approach you are likely to get a better price for the property. The buyer's agent also will be able to help a client who usually would have to wait to purchase.

Can a creative approach, like the contract of sale, be profitable to a real estate broker/agent and help him/her to bring in more business in this market?

The contract of sale if you understand it well will create more sales. Using the creative approach of the contract of sale will allow the agent/broker to be outside the box of conservative realtors that dominate the market. Remember, most agents unless you are well established or work for a large real estate firm cannot compete in a down market. The real estate broker/agent will get more listings, more sales and the contacts will increase for future business when the real estate market gets better.

How are the seller/vendor and buyer/vendee protected when using the contract of sale in a real estate transaction?

It is mandatory that if you are going to be creative and use the contract of sale or any other different approach to real estate you understand all of the concepts and rules. Enlist the services of a good title company to do the escrow and use a real estate attorney to either review or prepare the contract of sale. The title company will issue title insurance to the buyer/vendee and to the seller/vendor at the close of escrow.

The memorandum of contract of sale will be recorded. Demands on existing deeds of trust will be received, along with information as to where to make future payments, and what the property taxes are. Insurance, naming both parties, will be controlled by the collection company that will service the contract of sale. The supporting documents that will be signed and notarized are: a grant deed from seller/vendor to the buyer/vendee that will be held until the contract is satisfied and a quitclaim deed from buyer/vendee to seller/vendor in case of default.

WHAT TO LOOK FOR IN A CONTRACT OF SALE:

The items that go into a Contract of Sale transaction are as follows:

- Purchase Agreement
- Agency Agreement
- Addendums
- Appraisal
- Property Inspection

- Counter Offer (If Needed)
- Termite and Roof Report (If Needed)
- Insurance Policy on the Property
- Title and Escrow
- Beneficiary Statements on all underlying loans
- Current Property Tax Statement
- Memorandum of Contract of Sale
- Contract of Sale
- Grant Deed (Vendor-Vendee held)
- Quit Claim Deed (Vendee-Vendor held)
- Collection Agency Instructions (Payment Schedule)
- Set Up for future Exit Plan.

DOCUMENTS NEEDED FOR A CONTRACT OF SALE:

1. MEMORANDUM OF CONTRACT OF SALE

MEMORANDUM OF CONTRACT OF SALE

This Memorandum of Contract of Sale is intended to provide notice that (Name) , an unmarried man/woman Vendor (Seller) and (Name), husband and wife, Vendee (Buyer) have entered into an Contract of Sale, effective Month Day, Year with respect to the certain Real Property, commonly known as Address, City, California, with legal description of which is set forth in <u>Exhibit A</u>, hereto.

This Contract of Sale is effective as of the date on which the property becomes vested in the parties as Tenants-in-Common, and shall continue until the interest of one or both parties is sold, as provided in the Agreement.

Except as otherwise provided in the Contract of Sale, no party may assign, sell, transfer, hypothecate, or otherwise alienate any portion of his or her interest in the property, or the Contract of Sale, without the prior written consent of the other party. This Contract of Sale will terminate on Month Day, Year, unless extended by all parties.

_____   _____
Vendee   **Dated**

_____   _____
Vendor   **Dated**

Date _____
State of _____
County of _____

On _____ **Before me, (Name)** _____ ,
A Notary Public, in and for said state, personally appeared _____

who proved to me on the basis of satisfactory evidence to be the person(s) whose name(s) is/are subscribed to the within instrument and acknowledged to me that he/she/they executed the same in his/her/their authorized capacity(ies), and that by his/her/their signature(s) on the instrument the person(s) or the entity upon behalf of which the person(s) acted, executed the instrument.

I certify under PENALTY OF PERJURY under the laws of the State of California that the foregoing paragraph is true and correct.

WITNESS my hand and official seal.

Signature _____

_____
Name Typed or Printed

Sample Document

2. CONTRACT OF SALE (1 OF 6 PAGES)

CONTRACT OF SALE

THIS AGREEMENT, made and entered into this _____ day of <u>Month, Year,</u> by and between <u>Name, a married man/woman as his/her sole and separate property,</u> (Vendor's name), whose address is <u>Address, City, CA, Zip Code</u> (herein sometimes referred to as "Vendor"), and <u>Name, Vesting or Assignee</u> (Vendee's Name), whose address is <u>Address, City, CA Zip Code</u> (hereinafter sometimes referred to as "Vendee"); and <u>Title Company, a Corporation</u> (hereinafter sometimes referred to as "Trustee").

WITNESSETH:

WHEREAS, Vendor is now the owner of certain real property situated in the County of _____, State of California, commonly known as <u>Address, City, CA Zip Code</u> (property Street Address), and described as follows:

See Attached Exhibit "A"

WHEREAS, Vendor has agreed to sell, and Vendee has agreed to buy said real property on the terms and conditions hereinafter set forth;

WHEREAS, Vendor shall retain legal title in said real property until the Vendee can obtain proper financing to pay off existing first Deed of Trust on property.

NOW, THEREFORE, THE PARTIES HERETO DO HEREBY AGREE AS FOLLOWS:

PURCHASE PRICE

1. Vendor agrees to sell, and Vendee agrees to buy all of the aforedescribed real property for the sum of <u>Some Hundred Thousand Dollars</u> (Total purchase price) ($ <u>000,000.00</u>), lawful money of the United States, as hereinafter more fully set forth.

REQUEST FOR NOTICE OF DEFAULT/ SUBJECT TO EXISTING LOAN

2. In accordance with Section 2924b, Civil Code, request is hereby made by the undersigned Vendor and Vendee that a copy of any Notice of Default and a copy of any Notice of Sale under Deed of Trust recorded <u>Month Day, Year</u> in Book _____, Page _____, Document # <u>2005-0000000</u> , in <u>Some</u> County, California, as affecting above described property, executed by <u>name, a married man/woman as his/her sole and separate property</u> as Trustor in which <u>Some Corporation</u> is named as beneficiary, <u>Some Title</u> as Trustee, be mailed to Vendor and Vendee at addresses in paragraph 3 below.

1

Sample Document

CONTRACT OF SALE (2 OF 6 PAGES)

NOTICE AND REQUEST FOR NOTICE

3. Notices required or permitted under this agreement shall be binding if delivered personally to party sought to be served or if mailed by registered or certified mail, postage prepaid in the United States mail to the following:

Vendor: _____

Address: _____

Vendee: _____

Address: _____

PAYMENT OF PURCHASE PRICE

4. Vendee shall pay said purchase price of $ 000,000.00 as follows:

    (a) Vendee shall pay to Vendor the sum of $ 00,000.00 (Down Payment) as and for a down payment.

    (b) Vendor is not owed further equity, contract is being executed for the purpose of taking existing loan subject to, a collection will be set up to make monthly payments to Vendor, with proof given to Vendee of existing loan being paid.

    This Agreement will require 2 (Two) years to complete payment in accordance with its terms. Vendor shall make payment of any installments on existing First Deed of Trust in accordance with paragraph (c) herein below. Each such payment includes payment of the following items under the terms of said Note and Deed of Trust: Interest Only

    (c) The Vendor under this contract shall make due and timely payments of installments in the amount of $ 0000.00 interest on the First Deed of Trust and Note in the original amount of $ 000,000.00 in favor of Some Mortgage Company, the current unpaid balance of which is $ 000,000.00 with interest paid current.

    Vendor hereby indemnifies and agrees to save harmless Vendee from any default in connection with the obligation secured by the First, Second or Third Deeds of Trust. In the event any such installment payments on the obligations secured by said Deeds of Trust shall be in default, Vendee under this Contract may make payments thereof at his option and credit such payments to the obligation herein secured. In the event the Vendee makes a payment upon the Deeds of Trust which is in excess of the amount required to be made under this Contract, such excess shall

2

Sample Document

CONTRACT OF SALE (3 OF 6 PAGES)

be credited on the next installment or installment payments, which may become due under this Contract and Vendee shall not be required to pay such excess in addition to the regular payment of monthly installments under this contract.

(d) Upon recordation of The Memorandum of Contract, Vendor and Vendee will obtain policies of Title Insurance from <u>Title Company</u> with costs to be <u>split</u>.

(e) Tax estimates on which this Contract is based is the tax bill for fiscal year: <u>All property taxes starting January 1, 20XX will be paid by Vendee.</u>

(f) At any time Vendee may prepay without penalty all or any portion of balance due Vendor or on any other encumbrance on the property where the terms of such encumbrance so provide.

APPOINTMENT THE TITLE COMPANY

5. Upon recordation of the Memorandum of Contract, Vendor and Vendee irrevocably grant, transfer and assign their respective right, title and interest to the real property herein Some Title Company in Trust for purposes of holding an executed Grant Deed from Vendor to Vendee.
   (a) Power to convey to Vendee Legal Title upon full satisfaction of Vendee's obligation to Vendor, upon instructions from Vendor or his successor in interest.

TITLE INSURANCE

6. Upon recordation of the Memorandum of Contract, Some Title Company shall have cause to be issued a joint protection policy of title insurance (Lender's/ Owners) insuring the Vendor's (lender) and Vendee's (owner) interest herein.

POSSESSION

7. Vendee shall be entitled to possession of said real property upon recordation of the Agreement. Vendor's interest in the property is secured for payment of balance owed Vendor, and for performance of all terms and conditions to be performed by Vendee.

SOME TITLE COMPANY

8. The Title Companies duties shall consist of the following:
   (a) Should Vendee fail to perform under terms of this Agreement and thus be in default of any of its provisions including but not limited to payment of any insurance, taxes and indebtedness to existing lender or to prior encumbrancers, Vendor may declare all sums due, Vendor immediately

3

Sample Document

CONTRACT OF SALE (4 OF 6 PAGES)

due and payable by delivering to Some Title Company written declaration of default. Vendor shall deposit with Trustee this Contract, and all documents evidencing expenditures secured thereby.

DELIVERY OF GRANT DEED UPON VENDEE'S PERFORMANCE

9. Some Title Company, pursuant to the provisions of paragraph 5(a), or Vendor shall deliver to Vendee a Grant Deed of the above real property as hereinabove provided for, at such time as Vendee has lived up to all the terms of the contract and has secured financing to pay in full existing Deed of Trust on property.

TAXES

10. Vendee hereby assumes and agrees to pay before delinquency any and all taxes and assessments hereafter falling due on said real property. If Vendee shall fail to pay any of said taxes or assessments on or before the due date thereof, Vendor may at his option, declare a default under this Agreement or may pay said taxes and assessments and add any amounts so paid to the balance due Vendor under the terms of this Agreement. Any sums so paid by Vendor and added to the balance due under this Agreement shall bear interest at the rate provided for herein or the maximum interest rate provided by law, whichever is greater, until the same has been paid in full.

INSURANCE

11. Vendee further agrees that from and after Vendee assumes possession of said property, and until such time as all balances due to Vendor have been paid, Vendee shall keep the buildings and other improvements now and hereafter placed on said real property insured to the actual fair market value thereof against any loss by fire with an insurance company acceptable to Vendor and for the Vendor's benefit as his interest may appear; and shall provide public liability insurance on said property in reasonable amounts. Vendee agrees to pay all of the premiums thereof and to deliver copies of all policies and renewals thereof to Vendor. In the event the Vendee fails to provide such insurance or upon cancellation of such insurance, Vendor may obtain the insurance required by this paragraph and add to the balance due under this Agreement the amount of any premium thereof. Such added sum shall bear interest at the rate provided in paragraph 10 above.

MAINTENANCE

12. Vendee further agrees, until the purchase price hereof has been paid, that he will maintain all buildings and improvements now or hereafter on said real property in a good and habitable state of repair to maintain the value thereof and to pay when due all claims for labor performed and materials furnished thereof.

4

Sample Document

CONTRACT OF SALE (5 OF 6 PAGES)

RISK OF LOSS

13. After Vendee takes possession of said real property under the provisions of this Contract, Vendee assumes all hazards of damage to or destruction of any improvements now on said real property or hereafter placed thereon and of the taking of said real property, or any part thereof, for public use; and agrees that no such damage, destruction or taking shall constitute a failure of consideration under this Contract. In case any part of said real property is taken for public use, the portion of the condemnation award remaining after payment of reasonable expenses of procuring the same, shall be paid to Vendor and applied as payment on the purchase price hereunder or by payment to the beneficiary of a prior encumbrance as required by the terms of said encumbrance, unless said beneficiary and Vendor elect to allow the Vendee to apply all or a portion of such condemnation award to the rebuilding or restoration of any improvements damaged by such taking. In case of damage or destruction from a peril insured against, the proceeds of such insurance remaining after payment of the reasonable expenses of procuring the same, shall be devoted to the restoration or rebuilding of such improvements within a reasonable time unless the Vendee elects that said proceeds shall be paid to Vendor or prior encumbrancer.

TIME

14. Time is of the essence of this Agreement.

ATTORNEY FEES

15. If any party to this Agreement or any assignee of any party hereunder shall bring an action in any court of competent jurisdiction to enforce any covenant of this Agreement, including any action to collect any payment required hereunder, or to quiet his title against the other party to this Agreement, it is hereby mutually agreed that the prevailing party shall be entitled to reasonable attorney's fees and all costs and expenses in connection with said action, which sums shall be included in any judgment or decree entered in such action in favor of the prevailing party.

ASSIGNMENT OF CONTRACT

16. Vendee has the right to transfer, sell or assign his interest in the real property unless such transfer, sale or assignment may be consummated without acceleration of any senior encumbrance on the property. In the event of an acceleration of any senior encumbrance (by reason of a transfer, sale or assignment by the Vendee) the total amount of unpaid principal and interest due under this Contract shall be immediately due and payable to Vendor in, order to protect the Vendor against the loss of his security interest herein.

5

Sample Document

CONTRACT OF SALE (6 OF 6 PAGES)

BINDING EFFECT

17. This Agreement binds the parties hereto, their heirs, legatees, devisees, administrators, executors, successors and assignees.

CONSTRUCTION

18. All words used in this Agreement, including the words "Vendor" and "Vendee" shall be construed to include the plurals as well as the singular number and words used herein in the present tense shall include the future as well as the present, and words used in the masculine gender shall include the feminine and neuter gender.

19. This Agreement is not a "Standard Form Contract." Each party has participated in the negotiations leading to this document. Any presumption that an ambiguity in this Agreement should be construed against the drafting party is hereby waived.

IN WITNESS WHEREOF, the parties have hereunto executed this Agreement as of the date first above written.

_____   _____

_____   _____

VENDOR (S)   VENDEE (S)

Trustee hereby acknowledges and accepts the power hereinabove conferred, and agrees to act in accordance with the terms and conditions of this Contract of Sale.

Some Title Company

By _____   By _____

NOTE: THE PARTIES HERETO ARE CAUTIONED THAT, BY COMPLETING AND EXECUTING THIS AGREEMENT, LEGAL RIGHTS AND DUTIES ARE CREATED. THEY ARE ADVISED TO SEEK INDEPENDENT LEGAL COUNSEL AS TO ALL MATTERS CONTAINED IN THIS DOCUMENT.

6

Sample Document

3. GRANT DEED (HELD BY THIRD PARTY) – TO PROTECT THE "VENDEE"

RECORDED AT THE REQUEST OF:
Name

WHEN RECORDED MAIL TO:
Name
Address
City, CA Zip Code

DOCUMENTARY TRANSFER TAX $ _____

___ Computed on the consideration or value of property conveyed; OR
___ Computed on the consideration or value less liens or
     encumbrances remaining at time of sale

GRANT DEED

APN: 017-630-003

FOR A VALUABLE CONSIDERATION, receipt of which is hereby acknowledged,

Name of "Vendor"

hereby GRANT(S) to Name of "Vendee"

the real property in the City of   County of   , State of California   described as

SEE ATTACHED EXHIBIT "A"

Dated

STATE OF CALIFORNIA   } ss.
COUNTY OF ....   }   Name of Owner/"Vendor"

On ....
Before me, ... , a Notary Public
personally appeared ....
...., who proved to me on the basis of satisfactory evidence to be the person(s)
whose name(s) is/are subscribed to the within instrument and acknowledged to me that he/she/they executed the same in his/her/their authorized
capacity(ies), and that by his/her/their signature(s) on the instrument the person(s) or the entity upon behalf of which the person(s) acted, executed
the instrument.

I certify under PENALTY OF PERJURY under the laws of the State of California that the foregoing paragraph is true and correct.
WITNESS my hand and official seal.

Signature...

Sample Document

91

4. QUITCLAIM DEED (HELD BY THIRD PARTY) – TO PROTECT THE "VENDOR"

RECORDING REQUESTED BY:

When Recorded Mail Document and Tax Statement To:

Name
Address
City, CA Zip Code

APN: _____ SPACE ABOVE THIS LINE FOR RECORDER'S USE

QUITCLAIM DEED

The undersigned Grantor(s) declare(s)
Documentary transfer tax is $ _____ City Tax is $ _____
[   ]   Computed on full value of property conveyed, or
[   ]   Computed on full value less value of liens or encumbrances remaining at time
              of sale,
[   ]   Unincorporated Area

FOR A VALUABLE CONSIDERATION, receipt of which is hereby acknowledged,

Original Beneficiary / **"Vendee"**

hereby remises, releases and quitclaims to Name of **"Vendor"**

the following described real property in the County of _____ , State of California

DATED: _____

STATE OF CALIFORNIA
COUNTY OF_____
ON _____ before me,   Name OF "VENDEE"
_____, a Notary
Public, personally appeared _____
_____
_____   (Name)
who proved to me on the basis of satisfactory evidence to be the
person(s) whose name(s) is/are subscribed to the within instrument
and acknowledged to me that he/she/they executed the same in
his/her/their authorized capacity(ies), and that by his/her/their
signature(s) on the instrument the person(s) or the entity upon
behalf of which the person(s) acted, executed the instrument.

I certify under PENALTY OF PERJURY under the laws of the State
of California that the foregoing paragraph is true and correct.
WITNESS my hand and official seal.

Signature _____

Sample Document

CHAPTER EIGHT

LOWERING YOUR MORTGAGE PAYMENT— "LOAN MODIFICATION"

Changing the terms of your home loan by having it rewritten by your current lender is one of the ways to help you hold onto your property. Any homeowner who has suffered the loss of his/her job, a reduction of income, or a decline in their property value is going to need some kind of help to survive.

A year ago most lenders were very strict and would not have even considered a request from a consumer to rewrite or renegotiate his/her loan. The response would have been, "Either pay your loan payment on time or we will foreclose." The change has come about because of the downturn in the economy and the negative press that has overshadowed the loan industry.

Rewriting a loan will allow the homeowner to stay in his/her property with the plan of eventually surviving the downturn in the real estate market. When you approach your lender with the idea of rewriting your loan in order for it to be successful you must be sure that you can comfortably afford the new payment.

Most homeowners who try to work with a lender find it almost impossible to get through all of the red tape. The frustration of the duplication of paperwork or being put on hold for endless amounts of time becomes almost unbearable. Another problem is that lenders will almost always start the foreclosure process while they are rewriting your loan making the time factor even more crucial.

My advice is to seek professional help and arrange for a "loan modification company" to assist you. A professional will know how to work the system and can streamline the process — reducing the usual three-month time period to approximately sixty days. The loan modification company might also be able to get you a better interest rate with less cost and will also have the ability to underwrite the loan.

Let's examine what lenders look for when considering a loan rewrite/modification. The existing lender will want the modified payment to be comfortable and affordable for the consumer and will be looking at all of the financial statements of the property owner.

What will the lender need?

- Pay stubs
- Bank statements
- Proof of employment
- Proof of income and other income (child support, room rental)

The lender will also take into consideration the hardship or reasons why the homeowner fell behind in his/her payment. And if the rewrite/modification is granted will the homeowner be able to afford the new payment?

What are some examples/reasons for the delinquency?

- Job loss
- Loss of income
- Adjustment in mortgage payment.
- Divorce
- Illness

As the mortgage crisis escalates lenders have finally realized that if they are willing to rewrite loans this will result in less foreclosures. Bad loans, write-offs and short sales all go against the lender's bottom line for success.

Lenders will not modify a new loan to an ARM (Adjustable Loan). The new terms must be a five-year fixed loan with an "interest only" minimum payment. This will ensure that the homeowner can afford the mortgage payment.

Most lenders will require at least 3% of the back (delinquent) mortgage payments prior to doing the loan modification. The problem is that most homeowners do not have the $3,000 to $5,000 needed to finalize the loan rewrite.

My company, the Equity Share Group, has formed a non-profit corporation, "Happy Home Solutions," that will assist property owners in qualifying for loan rewrites. The money comes from grants donated by large banks, small lenders and credit unions. The reason these institutions are willing to participate is to help homeowners but it's also for the positive publicity.

When trying to get a lender to rewrite/modify your loan it is necessary to get your loan payment as low as possible. When making a payment adjustment the lender must take many factors into consideration:

- What interest rate did the lender sell the borrower on the original loan?

- How much has the property decreased in value?

- What is the financial strength of the borrower?

- How much of payment can the property owner afford?

Typically, the Lender would like to see at least 1% higher yield than what they sold the original loan for.

The bottom line is unless more loans are re-negotiated the real estate economy will not recover and the $700-billon bail-out package will not help consumers. By rewriting loans, stopping foreclosures, and making it possible for people to hold onto their homes consumer confidence will grow and the economy will begin to recover.

The Equity Share Group recently helped a single mother with two children reduce her mortgage payments from $2,650 down to $1,900 a month. This loan rewrite will allow this homeowner to stay in her home for the next five years.

Loan modification works if done for the right reasons. The process needs to be streamlined and more helpful to the consumer. Most homeowners who are behind in their mortgage payments do not understand the process and need help. The Equity Share Group's "Happy Home Solutions" can help and has been able to get lenders to do rewrites/modifications in just sixty days.

Homeowners do not need to be delinquent in their payments to apply for a loan rewrite/modification. The final outcome of a loan modification is to lower the payment, help the homeowner, and reduce the stress of owning a home in today's economy. Without loan rewrites the following chapters will define the property owner's future.

CHAPTER NINE

THE CONCEPT OF THE SHORT SALE

In today's real estate market where property values have declined by 20% to 40% and loan obligations on real estate have risen due to negative amortization the perfect alternative to foreclosure has become popular. The "short sale" approach is a sales transaction subject to a lender's approval in which the lender consents to a sale of the security interest in a property for less than what is owed on the note and accepts the proceeds in full satisfaction of the loan amount.

The short sale has been around for over 20 years in different variations but, because of the drastic affect of sub-prime loans, lenders are now willing to work with the discount process.

We have done a number of short sales over the past eight months. From practical experience the process is time consuming and not easy. Unlike a foreclosure that has set guidelines the short sale timeline is very vague, and requires a lot of paperwork and preparation on behalf of the borrower/seller. The borrower/seller must have a ready buyer and all of the paperwork prepared to submit to the lender.

When a borrower/seller is no longer in the position to make the mortgage payment, is facing foreclosure, and the current market value of the property, including title costs, commissions, repairs and back taxes, is less than the loan on the property, the borrower/seller may consider a short sale. The lender would consider a short sale because of the savings from the expense of foreclosure and from having another bank/real estate owned (REO) property on their books. The borrower/seller could look at the short sale in two ways: one is that it prevents a foreclosure on their credit history, and secondly, it releases them from an obligation that they can no longer afford.

A major reason why short sales fail is the length of time it takes to get the lender's approval. Most buyers are not willing to wait for months when trying to purchase a home. The real estate agent needs to put together a complete package when submitting an offer under a short sale thereby minimizing the long delays.

One of the newer approaches to dealing with lenders in the current real estate market is the "short sale." Lenders have the option to decide whether to take back a property through foreclosure or to work out an agreement that will allow the borrower to sell his/her property through the short sale process.

Let's look at an example of how the short sale process works. In 2004, I put a couple into a home in Pinole, California, with the help of an investor. The property was worth $650,000, with a first deed of trust for $480,000, and a second deed of trust for $110,000. My investor did an "equity share/joint ownership" with the couple for a contribution of $65,000. The investor's ownership was for 50%, with certain terms and conditions.

For the first two years everything was fine and all parties were living up to the terms and conditions. In 2007, the couple got a divorce and decided to vacate the property. I arranged a work-out between all parties as to how the investment would be maintained, and allow for all parties to have an exit plan.

I had the investor write an offer to the first deed of trust as a discount/short sale. The negotiated offer was for $320,000, which was almost a 40% discount over the original price of the home. Secondly, I negotiated with the second deed of trust and got them to take only a $5,000 payoff for their $110,000 obligation so the investor/co-owner was able to take back the property for a total of $325,000. The out-of-pocket advancement was $32,500 (10%), and the new first deed of trust payment was only $1,900 a month.

I was able to get the property back at a discount lease option the property for $2,400 a month and get a $5,000 option money deposit. The end result was a positive of $300 a month and in three to five years the owner/investor will get his original investment back plus a small return. This was a great outcome because the owner/investor did not lose his investment and will get tax benefits during the lease option time period. The original buyer/

occupants lost the property and got a divorce—but at least their credit was not completely destroyed.

Short sales have become more common today than they were eight months ago because lenders do not want to take properties back. The lenders have realized that it is much better to negotiate so that they can salvage the upside.

The end result of this example shows that an investor can hold onto his/her investment and can also salvage their original contribution with the possibility of some kind of upside.

Long-term, the investor can profit, and the original buyer/occupant who is losing the home can at least take the short sale and get the hardship tax exemption for the deficiency in losing their property.

Is a short sale for everyone? No, the buyer/occupant of the property must analyze the situation carefully and make sure the bank's short sale amount will benefit their position. The consequences of losing a property must be evaluated, not only because you are vacating the property, but because you have to also take into consideration the tax consequences.

Today, lenders are open to working with home owners that are unable to maintain their mortgage payments. The lenders have come to the conclusion that instead of fighting the borrower it is in their best interest to work with all parties.

The short sale has become a viable avenue for the consumer who cannot afford to stay in his/her property because the payments are too high and the lender who has the possibility of maintaining a loan by consolidating it instead of having to completely write it off.

Another example involves one of my investors who did an "equity share/ joint ownership" in a Roseville, California property. The investor bought into the property valued at $750,000. The Investor's contribution was $75,000 (10%). The equity share went along fine until the buyer/occupants stopped making the mortgage payment to the first lien holder. After several attempts at trying to work things out with the buyer/occupants the investor was forced to foreclose on the home to protect his investment.

The first lien holder demanded monthly payments and also started a foreclosure against the buyer/occupants. Through the foreclosure process taking approximately 111 to 120 days (non-Judicial), the investor was forced to take the property back with a trustee's deed. Because the owner/lien holder would not cooperate on a regular short sale with the lender, the investor had to go through with the foreclosure, take the property back, then apply for a "short payoff." A short payoff is roughly the same as a short sale but is a little more difficult to achieve.

The end result was, after over seven months of negotiating with the first deed of trust lender, we were able to reduce the first mortgage from $480,000 down to $320,000. Over the same time we talked the second deed of trust lender, who's loan amount was originally $75,000, into taking only $5,000. My investor now owns the home for a total value of $325,000. The current appraisal is $480,000, and we were able to lease option the home at the $480,000 value with lease payments that are giving the investor a great return.

The original owner/occupants lost the property due to non-payment and their refusal to cooperate. The investor had to take the property back to protect his original investment of $75,000, and in three years the investor will not only get his initial contribution back but will hopefully make a profit.

The short sale and short payoff are alternative approaches that can allow someone who is losing his/her home a way to get out from under it using these programs. It does hurt your credit but will allow you through the current "hardship rule" to go on with your life. At least now investors who need to protect their obligation have alternative methods to save their investments.

The one positive thing about a short sale for an owner/occupant is that if it works their credit will be hurt but at least they will not have a foreclosure against them. And they will have the benefit of living on the property approximately six months versus the four month time period of the foreclosure process. If the owner/occupant qualifies for a hardship because of losing their property they will not suffer the debt relief 1099 consequences that will affect their tax status.

Let's ask some questions that will define and clarify the different aspects of the "Short Sale."

What are the hardships required before a lender will approve a short sale?

Most lenders will require the seller to provide a valid hardship reason why a seller must sell at this time instead of staying in the home and waiting for the real estate market to recover. Many lenders will require the seller to formally write a hardship letter stating the reasons why they need to sell at this time.

What are the benefits of a short sale to the seller?

To the seller, the short sale will lower the debt enough to sell the property without the seller adding cash. It also avoids foreclosure and the negative affect on the seller's credit.

What are the benefits of a short sale to the lender?

It allows the lender to avoid having an REO (write-off) and being able to avoid a foreclosure may save money over the full claim payment.

What are some of the reasons the seller can put down as a hardship?

Lost job, divorce, debt, illness, death and salary decrease are all hardships.

Should the seller approach the lender about a short sale before putting his/her home on the market?

Approach the lender before you put your home on the market. Find out who handles short sales (loan mitigation, short sale, or workout department).

If you get an offer on a short sale what should the offer include before it is submitted?

First, there should be a contingency in the offer, stating the seller's capability to obtain a short sale agreement from the lender. Second, there should be a statement saying that the buyer understands that the closing could take longer than normal due to the need to obtain a short sale agreement from the lender. Third, when estimating the seller's shortage normal distribution of closing costs should be used (do not over estimate).

What is the complete package the lender will require to accept the short sale offer?

Generally, the following items will need to be submitted:

- Documented hardship letter
- Signed purchase agreement
- Loan approval letter on buyer
- Certified copy of the buyer's and seller's escrow instructions
- Preliminary report
- Proof of the buyer's financial condition
- CMA from a reputable real estate broker
- Authorization that the seller will not receive any money
- Attach comps and photos of the subject property

What does the lender look at in making a decision on a short sale?

The lender will look at the estimated cost of the foreclosure, and the REO Resale costs, then decide which is best option — accept the short sale proposal, or foreclose and resell the property.

What options does a lender have on a debt in California if the seller does not make the payments on the loan?

A lender may foreclose on the defaulting seller's real property that secures the loan (non-judicial or judicial foreclosures).

What other options may the lender consider instead of foreclosure?

The following options are open to the lender instead of foreclosure:

- Loan workout
- Deed in lieu of foreclosure
- Short sale
- Short pay-off

What is a Loan Workout?

Basically, a "loan workout" is a loan modification of the terms, such as a change in interest rate, payment schedule, and/or forgiving a portion of the debt.

What is a Deed in Lieu of Foreclosure?

This does not happen often but it's where the borrower/seller voluntarily delivers title to the lender for consideration and the lender accepts the property as paid-in-full. Lenders must be careful because other existing liens (junior) on the property do not get wiped out like they would in a foreclosure.

What is a Short Payoff?

A "short payoff" is when the lender accepts less than the remaining mortgage amount, as full payment of the loan. The property need not be sold.

What is a Deficiency Judgment?

A "deficiency judgment" is a judgment obtained by the lender in court against the seller for the difference between the unpaid balance of the secured debt and the amount produced by sale or the fair market value of the security whichever is greater in a judicial foreclosure. You can only get a deficiency judgment using a judicial foreclosure.

Under California law (Anti-Deficiency Status) are certain borrowers protected from the Deficiency Judgment?

The following situations will prohibit a deficiency judgment:

- Purchase money
- Seller carry back
- Trustee's sale (non-judicial foreclosure)
- Three-Month time limit
- Fair value limitations

Can a lender avoid the foreclosure process and just sue the borrower on the note?

No. A lender cannot sue on a debt secured by a trust deed except for a judicial foreclosure.

Why would a lender agree to accept a short sale?

The cost of doing the foreclosure, risk of destruction of the property, and lender owned REOs may take a long time to sell.

Does the short sale affect a defaulting seller's credit rating?

Yes. Lenders will report the short sale as being settled for less than full payoff. This will show up as a negative on the credit report although not as negative as a foreclosure where the loan is written off by the lender.

When a seller is late with payments and a notice of default is filed on the property does this affect the seller's credit?

Yes. The lender will report payments that are late for 30, 60, 90 or more days after the due date; this will harm the borrower's credit.

Is the method lenders use to report a short sale a negotiable item?

Usually not. The short sale is usually reported to a credit reporting agency as settled for less than the full balance. You can negotiate to have this dismissed from the credit agency.

Are there any tax effects of a short sale?

Yes. The tax implications for the seller could be so significant that a short sale would not be in the seller's best interest. Before a short sale is contemplated, it is strongly recommended that the seller seek the advice of a CPA. The IRS is allowing special hardship cases to have an exemption as to being given a 1099-C for reporting debt relief due to a short sale.

What documentation does the seller need to give to the lender to prove that there is a hardship in qualifying for a short sale?

The seller will need to provide the following documents to show a hardship. These documents will then be included with the other documents obtained from the realtor, title company, and the new lender for the buyer.

- Completed and signed IRS Form 4506 (Request a copy of the Tax form)
- Completed and signed personal financial worksheet
- Tax returns for the past 2 years
- Employment paycheck stubs for the past 2 years
- Profit and Loss Statement (self-employed)
- Bank statements for the past 3 months

Does the lender "Workout Department" need a purchase agreement to accompany the other documentation?

Yes. A purchase agreement that is signed by both the seller and the buyer, for the amount the buyer wants to pay. This offer is often rejected until a satisfactory purchase price is agreed upon by the lender.

DOCUMENTS NEEDED FOR A SHORT SALE:

1. SELLER'S WRITTEN AUTHORIZATION FOR AGENT TO TALK TO THE BANK

SELLER/ BORROWER NAME
Address
City, State Zip Code
Phone Number

Month Day, Year

Mortgage Company/Lender
Address
City, State Zip Code
Loan Number: 12345678910
Balance: $000,000
SSN: XXX-XX-XXXX

To Whom It May Concern:

This letter is to verify that I am working with the Company/Agent Name, to get all of the loan information and obligations in order, for my property, located at Address, City, State. Please know that I authorize the release any, and all, loan information to Agent Name, at Company Name. His/her information is as follows:

Name
Company
Address
City, State Zip Code
Phone Number
Fax Number
Cell Number

Your immediate attention to this matter will be greatly appreciated. Thank you, and please call me if you have any questions.

Sincerely,

Seller/Borrower Name

2. HANDWRITTEN HARDSHIP LETTER FROM SELLER

SELLER/BORROWER NAMES
Address
City, State Zip Code
Phone Number

DATE: Month Day, Year

SUBJECT: MORTGAGE FOR ADDRESS, CITY, STATE
             LOAN NUMBER: 000000000000

ATTEN: LENDER/SAVINGS AND LOAN COMPANY

TO WHOM IT MAY CONCERN:

First of all, we want to thank you for taking the time to look over our loan and helping us with the situation we're in. We are very happy with our Lender/Savings and Loan Company Name loan, and our loan is in good standing, but, due to our situation, we are having a difficult time keeping up the payment we are currently making.

Seller/Borrower Name has been laid off, and is presently unemployed. Name is looking for a job, and hopes to be employed again soon. I have a good job, and I have been trying to pay all of our household expenses. Needless to say, with only one income, we are struggling. We are also taking care of a sick, live-in relative, which adds additional expense and stress to our already stressful situation.

We love our home and we want to keep it, and we will do whatever it takes to make that happen. Is there anything you can do to adjust our loan to a more affordable payment, so we can stay afloat during this difficult time?

We ask that you please consider our situation and work with us. Your immediate attention to this matter will be greatly appreciated. Again, thank you for your time, and we look forward to hearing from you soon.

Sincerely,

Husband and Wife Name

CHAPTER TEN

FORECLOSURE

Any person or entity that loans money secured by real estate, that uses a deed of trust and note has the right of a non-judicial foreclosure. The foreclosure will be initiated by some sort of violation of the terms and conditions of the agreement.

To understand your rights as a borrower/trustor you must understand and follow the rules that were set up in the deed of trust and note. Some of the covenants that make up the terms and conditions are as follows:

- Monthly payments
- Insurance
- Property taxes
- Condition of property
- Due on sale clause
- Pre-payment clause
- Late charge

As the borrower/trustor who borrowed the funds you agreed to follow certain rules. The lender/beneficiary, either an institution or individual, has the right to be paid back either monthly or deferred with interest. The terms must be legal and follow the standards that are allowed by the law.

The foreclosure (non-judicial) is a process that must follow a specific outline in order to be legal. Unfortunately most trustees (party holding the foreclosure) have a staff that is not always exact about following the necessary rules and documentation to qualify the process.

The benefit to the trustee handling the foreclosure is that most people losing their property to foreclosure do not fully understand the process so they never know whether the format is being followed in the right way or not.

Over the a twelve month period in 2008 to 2009 I was able to overturn approximately fifteen foreclosures. When I am hired by the trustor/borrower to help them understand the procedures it is my duty to see if they can find an alternative to help them get out from under their property.

When a trustee is appointed to hold the foreclosure procedure under the non-judicial foreclosure they must follow all rules stipulated by the law. A trustee must obtain certain documentation from the beneficiary (lender) as to why they want to take action against the trustor/borrower. The trustee will need the original deed of trust and note and will need evidence stating why the beneficiary is foreclosing. The trustee must follow the rights to registered notice of all parties.

The foreclosure process is not easy and must be very carefully documented. The trustee must continuously update the trustee sale guarantee report (TSG), must advertise, post, mail out, and follow a strict timeline that is crucial to the law. The sad thing is that most trustors/borrowers and their representatives never challenge what is right or wrong.

I have been able to overturn foreclosures for the following reasons:

- Timeframe for mailings of the notice of default
- Posting of the notice of trustee sale in two public places
- Registered letter to all parties for notice of trustee sale
- Advertising time periods
- Non-notification of IRS Liens
- Trustee's communications with all obligated parties

Stopping a foreclosure allows the trustor/borrower to have more time to sell his/her property before they lose it. It gives all parties more control of the process that is dictated by the beneficiary/lender.

Never be afraid of challenging the process so that you can either protect your investment, or at least buy yourself enough time to establish an approach that can solve your problems. If you ever need to analyze the foreclosure process, and want to make sure that the trustee has done everything in the right way then make sure you hire a professional who understands the pros and cons of the process.

Eventually if you are not able to find a solution you will lose the property to foreclosure.

When I represent an investor who has a deed of trust and note owed to him/her it is imperative that I do the right things to protect the investment. The beneficiary/lender is owed money, they are either getting monthly payments, or the obligation owed to them is deferred. When someone is owed money secured by a deed of trust you should always get title insurance, do some research on the individual who owes you the money, and examine the value of the security, through an appraisal. Also, be sure to understand the senior loans on the property that take priority over the obligation owed to you.

My tips to the investor who is owed money are check to make sure the senior deed of trust is current, make sure the that property taxes are being paid, make sure you are named as an additional insured party on the insurance policy, and always get title insurance.

If you find out that you are in jeopardy of default then immediately contact the borrower to see if you can work out the problem. If the senior note is in default then immediately seek advice about starting foreclosure on your obligation. Do not wait for a long period of time to react. Foreclosure is a tool to protect your investment, it should not be abused but remember when the person who owes you money does not contact you about his/her payment problems, then you must take action.

SECURITY FOR MONEY LOANED IN MOST WESTERN STATES IS THE DEED OF TRUST AND NOTE SO WHAT ARE SOME OF THE MOST ASKED QUESTIONS ABOUT THE FORECLOSURE PROCESS?

What is a Deed of Trust?

Basically a "deed of trust" is a contract between the person or entity that borrows and the person or entity that loans funds secured by Real estate the Borrower owns. The property is the security for the payment. The real definition is a voluntary lien on the property owned by the borrower/trustor.

Once signed and notarized, is the Deed of Trust usually recorded?

Yes. Without recording the document (in the County where the property is located) the security does not exist. Priority of recording (date) chronological order determines the lender/beneficiary's position. Without recording the deed of trust you cannot foreclose under the non-judicial laws.

What is a Note?

A "note" is an unsecured document that defines the terms and conditions of money loaned. The note states things like the interest rate, timeline for the loan, late charges, Due on sale clause, prepayment, adjustable rates, and the general terms and conditions. The person who owes the money is referred to as the "payer" and the lender is referred to as the "payee."

For a Deed of Trust to be valid does it have to have a Note included?

Yes. The note that goes with the deed of trust must state all the terms and conditions. The security for the note is the deed of trust. The security for the deed of trust is the real estate pledged to be recorded. A note that is not secured by a deed of trust is not secured (e.g., a note to a friend for $500 or a note secured by an automobile).

Do all States use a Deed of Trust to secure liens on property for money loaned?

No, many eastern states use mortgages, not deeds of trust. There is a distinct difference.

What is the difference between a Deed of Trust and a Mortgage?

The main difference is the parties named in the documents and the procedure to take the property back if the obligation is violated.

Who are the parties that make up the Deed of Trust?

There are three parties that make up the deed of trust.

> **Trustor** – The party who borrows the money, owes the money to the lender/beneficiary. The borrower of the money must own the property that is being secured or be in the process of purchasing it.

> **Trustee** – The trustee is the third party on the deed of trust. Under California law the trustee has two powers: the power of sale (foreclosure), and the power to re-convey (payoff, or satisfaction of the loan) (e.g., the trustee could be the title company, the escrow company, an attorney, or a corporation that does that type of business).

> **Beneficiary** – The beneficiary is the lender and can be an institutional lender or a private lender, etc.

What is an Assignment of a Deed of Trust?

An assignment of a deed of trust is a transfer of all rights and lender/beneficiary to another entity (must be recorded).

What is a Substitution of Trustee?

A substitution of trustee is when all lenders/beneficiaries transfer rights from one trustee to another (this must be recorded).

What are the reasons a Lender/Beneficiary can start foreclosure or take action against a Borrower for default?

Examples of default are the following:
- Default on monthly payments
- Failure to keep insurance on the property
- Failure to keep property taxes current

- Failure to keep the property up
- Due on dale (selling property without acknowledgment from the lender/beneficiary)
- One failure to keep senior loans current

When you loan money, is it necessary to obtain the following documentation?

- Title Report
- Credit Report
- Insurance/Additional Insured
- Payment schedule on a Senior Deed of Trust
- Value through Appraisal

Yes. To protect your money it is essential that you do all of the above. Only lend money to people who own the property — 100% ownership should be considered. Make sure the entity or person who borrows the money is credit-worthy and has the financial means to make the payments. Make sure you are insured and that the property value is protected. Finally you must be able to check to see that the borrower is paying the senior obligation and that the property has adequate value to protect the loan.

What is a Foreclosure?

A foreclosure is the non-judicial right on a deed of trust under the State of California to take action on your obligation. The rules and laws are spelled out as to what you can and cannot do under the process.

As the Beneficiary/Lender how do I show the First Right of Default?

Under the non-judicial foreclosure the lender/beneficiary must show reason why they want to foreclose:

MONETARY
- Default on payment
- Default on balloon payment

- Non-payment of property taxes
- Cancellation of insurance

NON-MONETARY
- Destruction of property
- Violation of the due on sale clause

Who does the Foreclosure?

The trustee either the original trustee or a substituted trustee acts as the agent to do the foreclosure.

What items and actions do the Trustee need to start a Foreclosure?

The following items are needed to start a foreclosure:
- Authorization from the lender/beneficiary
- The original note and deed of trust
- Substitution of trustee, if needed
- Declaration of default (reason for foreclosure)
- Fee to start the foreclosure
- Approval to record the notice of default

What document does the Trustee need to record in order to start the Foreclosure?

The notice of default is the document that is publicly filed against the property owner. The reasons for filing this document are: a missed payment or other covenants that have been defaulted on. This document must be recorded in the County where the property is located.

When you initiate a Foreclosure do you need a Title Report from the Title Company to give you evidence of the current status of the subject property?

The report you need when involved with a foreclosure is called a Trustee Sale Guarantee Report (TSG). This report gives you all of the information a preliminary report states as well as any additional liens anything affecting title including the addresses and phone numbers of all and the foreclosure procedures.

Is there another reason for the TSG other than the above?

The TSG after the issuance of the trustee's deed allows the lender/beneficiary to eventually give title insurance to a new buyer.

What is the difference between a Deed of Trust that has "Recourse" and one that is "Non-Recourse"?

"Recourse" means that the lender/beneficiary has the right to go after other assets the trustor owns if there is not enough value in the property. "Non-recourse" means that the lender/beneficiary has to rely on the value of the property secured to get his/her obligation paid off.

During the Foreclosure process, at what time period does the Trustor lose the right to pay all delinquencies before the sale takes place?

In the 1990s, the State of California, under non-judicial foreclosure, allowed the trustor to reinstate the loan within five days of the day of sale. If the trustor fails to exercise his/her right then the lender/beneficiary has the right to call the entire balance due plus all costs and fees.

If an IRS Lien is recorded against the property does the Deed of Trust that is being Foreclosed on (the Senior Lien), wipe out the IRS Lien?

The IRS has a redemption period of 120 days after the trustee's deed is recorded. This is only in affect if the IRS lien is recorded within twenty-five days of the actual sale.

Can a Lender/Beneficiary advise the Trustee to postpone a Foreclosure at anytime and after proper notice resume the Foreclosure?

Yes, the trustee upon instructions from the lender/beneficiary can postpone the foreclosure as long as it is before the advertising stage. If the lender/beneficiary postpones the sale within the advertising time period before the final sale then it might be necessary to re-advertise before another date and sale take place.

What is the time period for a Non-Judicial Foreclosure?

The Ten Steps for a Foreclosure timeline are:

Day 1 – Record notice of default

Within 10 Days – Mail conformed copies of the notice of default (USPS return receipt) to the trustor and special requests

Within 3 Months – Trustee's sale/setting the sale date

Within 5 Days of Sale – Right of trustor to reinstate the loan

Sale Date – Public Auction

A non-judicial foreclosure usually takes 111 to 120 Days.

If there are no bidders the lender/beneficiary gets the property back.

To convey property back to the lender/beneficiary use a trustee's deed.

What are the duties of the Trustee when preparing for a Foreclosure Sale?

The trustee must prepare the following documentation:

- Declaration of Default
- Notice of Default
- Statement of Default
- Trustee Sale Guarantee (Title Company)
- Substitution of Trustee if needed
- Mailings – Certified to all parties
- Publication – Prepare for publication on the 90th Day

- Record Notice of Trustee's Sale
- Publish Notice of Trustee's Sale
- Postings
- Hold Sale – Record Trustee's Deed to the highest bidder

What happens at the Foreclosure Sale?

The sale is held with publication and goes to the highest bidder unless the lender/beneficiary decides to postpone the sale, accept a lower bid, or extend the foreclosure.

Things that can happen at a Foreclosure Sale:

- Auction with the agreed upon beneficiary bid
- Auction to the highest bidder
- Suspension of the sale
- Trustor declares bankruptcy and stops the sale
- Sale happens and a trustee's deed goes to the highest bidder

What happens when a Trustee's Deed is executed upon the Sale?

All junior liens are eliminated or cancelled. Junior IRS liens are put on hold and are subject to a redemption period of 120 days. The sale is taken subject to the senior lien encumbrances. The new owner must evict the tenants, owners, or occupants through an eviction process.

What is the Judicial Foreclosure?

A "judicial foreclosure" is basically a court action. An attorney will take action for the delinquency of money owed. The cost is quite a bit more than the non-judicial foreclosure and the process takes four times the normal time period.

Why do a Judicial Foreclosure versus a Non-Judicial Foreclosure?

There are two main reasons to use a judicial foreclosure:

- Right to a deficiency judgment
- Diversification to after other assets of the borrower

What are the disadvantages of doing a Judicial Foreclosure?

It costs more to do a judicial foreclosure (e.g., a non-judicial foreclosure would cost about $2,000 to $2,500 total and a judicial foreclosure would take seven to eight months with a cost of $10,000, or more). Finally the judicial foreclosure has a "right of redemption."

On the East Coast and in certain other States, Mortgages are used instead of Deeds of Trust. What are the differences?

Mortgages do not have a Trustee.

- No power of sale
- No power to re-convey
- No short-term foreclosure

What is a Deficiency Judgment?

A "deficiency judgment" means that if the lender/ beneficiary forecloses and the property taken back has no real equity value then the lender/beneficiary has the right under the judicial foreclosure to go after additional properties owned by the trustor/borrower to attempt to collect his/her debt.

Can you purchase a Deed of Trust/Note and have it assigned to you with all rights and conditions?

Yes, the document known as an "assignment of deed of trust" with proper acknowledgment will give all rights to the new lender/beneficiary.

When a Deed of Trust is paid off, or satisfied what document is needed to remove it from title?

To satisfy and remove the deed of trust from the records (payoff), a re-conveyance is used (and must be recorded).

The foreclosure process is common in today's market. The right of lender/beneficiaries to take action is built into the terms and conditions of the note and deed of trust.

Most institutional lenders allow three to five months of monthly payments to be delinquent before taking action to foreclose.

The lender/beneficiaries that hold a second or third deed of trust on a property will usually start foreclosure on the property much earlier than the institutional lender.

Most trustors if given the opportunity would not want to have a foreclosure process taken against them. Trustors can do a number of things to either negotiate, change, or stop the action of foreclosure.

If the trustor is in the military (active), then the lender/beneficiary cannot foreclose on the trustor. If the lender/beneficiary declares bankruptcy then the foreclosure will become frozen until released.

THE FOLLOWING COMMON DOCUMENTS ARE USED IN THE FORECLOSURE PROCESS

SECURITY DOCUMENTS:

1. Deed of Trust
2. Note
3. Substitution of Trustee
4. Assignment of Deed of Trust

FORECLOSURE DOCUMENTS:

1. Declaration of Default
2. Notice of Default
3. Letter
4. Notice of Trustee's Sale
5. Trustee's Deed Upon Sale

SECURITY DOCUMENTS NEEDED FOR A FORECLOSURE:

1. DEED OF TRUST

in Orange County August 17, 1964, and in all other counties August 18, 1964, in the book and at the page of Official Records in the office of the county recorder of the county where said property is located, noted below opposite the name of such county, namely.

COUNTY	BOOK PAGE	PAGE	COUNTY	BOOK	PAGE	COUNTY	BOOK	PAGE	COUNTY	BOOK	
Alameda	1288	556	Kings	858	713	Placer	1028	379	Sierra	38	187
Alpine	3	130-31	Lake	437	110	Plumas	166	1307	Siskiyou	506	762
Amador	133	438	Lassen	192	367	Riverside	3778	347	Solano	1287	621
Butte	1330	513	Los Angeles	T-3678	874	Sacramento	5039	124	Sonoma	2067	427
Calaveras	185	338	Madera	911	136	San Benito	300	405	Stanislaus	1970	56
Colusa	323	391	Marin	1849	122	San Bernardino	6213	768	Sutter	655	585
Contra Costa	4684	1	Mariposa	90	453	San Francisco	A-804	596	Tehama	457	183
Del Norte	101	549	Mendocino	667	99	San Joaquin	2855	283	Trinity	108	595
El Dorado	704	635	Merced	1660	753	San Luis Obispo	1311	137	Tulare	2530	108
Fresno	5052	623	Modoc	191	93	San Mateo	4778	175	Tuolumne	177	160
Glenn	469	74	Mono	69	302	Santa Barbara	2065	881	Ventura	2607	237
Humboldt	801	83	Monterey	357	239	Santa Clara	6626	664	Yolo	769	16
Imperial	1189	701	Napa	704	742	Santa Cruz	1638	607	Yuba	398	693
Inyo	165	672	Nevada	363	94	Shasta	800	633			
Kern	3756	690	Orange	7182	18	San Diego SERIES 5 Book 1964, Page 149774					

shall inure to and bind the parties hereto, with respect to the property above described. Said agreements, terms and provision contained in said subdivisions A and B, (identical in all counties, and printed on Pages 3 and 4 hereof) are by the within reference thereto, incorporated herein and made a part of this Deed of Trust for all purposes as fully as if set forth at length herein, and Beneficiary may charge for a statement regarding the obligation secured hereby, provided the charge therefore does not exceed the maximum allowed by law.

hereunder be mailed to him at his

WHEN RECORDED MAIL TO

Name
Address
City, CA Zip Code

SPACE ABOVE THIS LINE FOR RECORDER'S USE

DEED OF TRUST WITH ASSIGNMENT OF RENTS
(SHORT FORM)

This DEED OF TRUST, made Month Day, between Name/Company Name, a California Corporation herein called TRUSTOR,

whose address is: Address, City, CA Zip Code

CHOSEN TITLE INSURANCE COMPANY, a California Corporation, herein called TRUSTEE, and

Trust Company of Choice, Inc. FBO (name) IRA #   herein called BENEFICIARY

WITNESSETH: That Trustor grants to Trustee in trust, with power of sale, that property in the
City of   Same City   County of   Same County,   State of California, described as

SEE ATTACHED EXHIBIT "A"

together with the rents, issues and profits thereof, subject, however, to the right, power and authority hereinafter given to and conferred upon Beneficiary to collect and apply such rents, issues and profits for the Purpose of Securing (1) payment of the sum of $000,000.00, with interest thereon according to the terms of a Promissory Note or Notes of even date herewith made by Trustor, payable to order of Beneficiary, and extensions or renewals thereof, and (2) the performance of each agreement of Trustor incorporated by reference or contained herein (3) payment of additional sums and interest thereon which may hereafter be loaned to Trustor, or his successors or assigns, when evidenced by a Promissory Note or Notes reciting that they are secured by this Deed of Trust.

To protect the security of this Deed of Trust, and with respect to the property above described, Trustor expressly makes each and all of the agreements, and adopts and agrees to perform, and be bound by each and all of the terms and provisions set forth in Subdivision A, and it is mutually agreed that each, and all, of the terms and provisions set forth in Subdivision B of the fictitious Deed of Trust recorded.

(continued on the next page)   1159-5M (1/96)

to the within Instrument and
by his/her/their signature(s) on the

is true and correct.

official notarial seal)

2. NOTE

NOTE

On Month Day, Year, Name, Vesting (together with his permitted successors and assigns herein called "Borrower" promises to pay to the order of Name, Vesting (herein, together with his successors and assigns who become holders of this Note, ("Lender"), at City, California , or at such other place as may be designated by Lender, and at the times stated in this Note, the principal (Some Thousand Dollars) ($000,000.00) (or such lesser sum as may be advanced hereunder) together with interest on the outstanding principal balance and all accrued or deferred interest hereunder (collectively "Loan Balance") at the rates per annum set forth below (based on a 360-day year and charged for actual days elapsed).Property: Address, City, CA Zip Code.

Term of this Note will all be due and payable in full on Month Day, Year.

From the date of this Note, interest shall accrue on the Loan Balance at a rate equal to Some percent (00%). Accrued but unpaid interest shall be added to principal on the maturity date of this Note. If property is sold, transferred without written consent of the Payee/Beneficiary, then the Note and Deed of Trust can be called due and payable by Payee/Beneficiary. This Note and Deed of Trust can be assigned to a new beneficiary under the same term and conditions as are stated in this document.

Both principal and interest shall be paid by Borrower in lawful money of the United States of America such that Lender has received immediately available funds for the credit of Borrower on the date that such payments are due. If Borrower defaults on Note and Deed of Trust, they will be responsible for all foreclosure, attorney and trustee fees to protect Lender.

This Deed of Trust and Note is for the purpose of securing a Joint Ownership Interest. The terms and covenants of this document are the same items 1 thru 30 in said Agreement dated Month Day, Year between Payee and Payor. Violations of the terms and conditions of the Agreement is deemed a default of this Note and secured Deed of Trust. This Note is part of the Joint Ownership Agreement as a Participating Note.

From and after the maturity date hereof, or such earlier date as the principal, interest and charges owing on this Note become due and payable, the whole of the principal, interest and charges owing on this Note shall thereafter bear interest, until paid in full.

This Note shall be construed and enforced in accordance with the laws of the State of Californi should default be made in payment of any installment of principal or in the performance of any obligation contained in Note by which this Note is secured, the whole sum of principal shall become immediately due at the option of the holder hereof principal payable in lawful money of the United States. Payor agrees to pay such sum as the court may fix as attorneys fees in said action.

_____   _____
Name   Name

3. SUBSTITUTION OF TRUSTEE

LEGAL DESCRIPTION

EXHIBIT "A"

THE LANS REFERRED TO HEREIN BELOW IS SITUATED IN THE CITY OF ANYCITY, COUNTY OF ANYCOUNTY, STATE OF CALIFORNIA AND IS DESCRIBED AS FOLLOWS:

A portion of Lots 1,2, and 3, as said lots are shown upon that certain Map entitled "Any Subdivision of Lots 12 and 34 exclusive, of Block 1, Some Tract, Anycity, California, filed Month Day Year in Book of Maps, Page 123, in the office of the County Recorder of Any County, bounded as follows:

Beginning at the point of intersection of the Western line of Any Street with the Northern line of Some Way, as said street and way are shown on said Map; running thence along the said last mentioned line South 90° 33' West (bearing South 90° 33' West being assumed for the purpose of this description) 90.00 feet; thence North 3° 44' West parallel with the said line of Any Street, 50.00 feet; thence North 90° 55' 50" East 90.00 feet; to a point on the said Western ... .00 feet from said point ...tern line of Any Street.

RECORDING REQUESTED BY:
Name

When Recorded Mail Document To:
Name
Address
City, CA Zip Code

SPACE ABOVE THIS LINE FOR RECORDER'S USE

ASSIGNMENT OF DEED OF TRUST

FOR VALUE RECEIVED, the undersigned hereby grants, assigns and transfers to

Name

all beneficial interest under that certain Deed of Trust dated Month Day, Year
executed by   Name,   Trustor,
to Name Title Insurance Company, a California Corporation, as Trustee
and recorded Month Day, Year as Instrument No.   in Book ---, Page ------ , of Official Records
in the County Recorder's Office of Contra Costa County, State of California, describing land therein as:

Address, City, California

See Attached Exhibit "A"

DATED:

STATE OF CALIFORNIA
COUNTY OF _____
ON _____ before me,
_____, a Notary Public
personally appeared
_____
_____   _____
                                                                                    Name

who proved to me on the basis of satisfactory evidence to be the person(s)
whose name(s) is/are subscribed to the within instrument and acknowledged
to me that he/she/they executed the same in his/her/their authorized capacity(ies),
and that by his/her/their signature(s) on the instrument the person(s) or the entity
upon behalf of which the person(s) acted, executed the instrument.

I certify under PENALTY OF PERJURY under the laws of the State of California
that the foregoing paragraph is true and correct.

WITNESS my hand and official seal.

Signature _____

FD-205 (Rev 9/94)   ASSIGNMENT OF DEED OF TRUST

4. ASSIGNMENT OF RENTS

SUBSTITUTION OF TRUSTEE

WHEREAS, , was the original Trustor,
was the original Trustee, and ,was the original Beneficiary, under that
certain Deed of Trust dated Month Day, Year and recorded Month Day, Year as Instrument No.

in Book– , Page– , Official Records of the County of , State of .

And WHEREAS, the undersigned is the present Beneficiary under said Deed of Trust , and

WHEREAS, the undersigned desires to substitute a new Trustee under said Deed of Trust in the place and stead
of said original Trustee thereunder.

Now therefore, the undersigned Beneficiary hereby substitutes **Company Name, dba Company Name, Inc,
a California Corporation**, whose address is Street, City, CA Zip Code as Trustee under said Deed of Trust.
Whenever the context hereof so requires, the masculine gender includes the feminine and/or neuter, and the
singular number includes the plural.

DATED:

STATE OF CALIFORNIA
COUNTY OF _____   By: _____
ON _____ before me,
_____, a Notary Public   By: _____
personally appeared _____

who proved to me on the basis of satisfactory evidence to be the
person(s) whose name(s) is/are subscribed to the within instrument
and acknowledged to me that he/she/they executed the same
in his/her/their authorized capacity(ies), and that by his/her/their
signature(s) on the instrument the person(s), or the entity upon
behalf of which the person(s) acted, executed the instrument.

I certify under PENALTY OF PERJURY under the laws of the State of California that the foregoing paragraph is true and correct.

Witness my hand and official seal.

Signature _____

FD-236 (Rev 9/94)   SUBSTITUTION OF TRUST

"FORECLOSURE" DOCUMENTS NEEDED FOR A FORECLOSURE:

1. DECLARATION OF DEFAULT

NAME

ADDRESS

ANY ADDITIONAL ADDRESSES

INFORMATION ABOUT THE PROPERTY

_____ VACANT LAND _____ SINGLE FAMILY RESIDENCE

_____ MULTIPLE FAMILY _____ COMMERCIAL/INDUSTRIAL

PROPERTY ADDRESS

ASSESSOR'S PARCEL NUMBER:

ADDITIONAL INFORMATION:

BY REASON OF THIS DEFAULT THE UNDERSIGNED, WHO IS THE BENEFICIARY/SERVICER, MAKES THIS DECLARATION OF DEFAULT AND ELECTS TO CAUSE THE TRUST PROPERTY TO BE SOLD TO SATISFY THE OBLIGATIONS SECURED BY THE TRUST DEED.

AS DULY AUTHORIZED AGENT FOR THE BENEFICIARY OR AS TRUSTEE UNDER SAID DEED OF TRUST, YOU ARE HEREBY AUTHORIZED AND DIRECTED TO FULLY COMPLETE AND RECORD SAID NOTICE OF DEFAULT, \AND TO PROCEED WITH A NON-JUDICIAL FORECLOSRUE SALE OF THE REAL PROPERTY DESCRIBED IN SAID DEED OF TRUST I/WE PROMISE AND AGREE TO PAY THE TRUSTEE'S FEE IN THE AMOUNT PERMITTED BY LAW, TOGETHER WITH ALL THE COSTS AND EXPENSES INCIDENTAL TO THESE PROCEEDINGS. IT IS ALSO AGREED ...

Network Foreclosure Services
390 Diablo Road, Suite 130
Danville, CA 94526
925.831.1250

AUTHORIZATION TO BEGIN FORECLOSURE PROCEEDINGS
AND DECLARATION OF DEFAULT

LOAN NO. / NAME

DOCUMENTS ENCLOSED

ORIGINAL   COPY

_____ NOTE _____

_____ DEED OF TRUST _____

_____ ASSIGNMENT _____

_____ MODIFICATION OF TERMS _____

_____ EXTENSION AGREEMENT _____

_____ OTHER _____

LOAN STATUS

UNPAID PRINCIPAL BALANCE $ _____ INTEREST RATE _____ %
PAYMENT WHICH BECAME DUE ON __/__/__ WAS NOT MADE
DATE INTEREST WAS PAID TO __/__/__
TOTAL AMOUNT OF MONTHLY INSTALLMENT $ _____
MONTHLY AMOUNT OF MONTHLY INSTALLMENT $ _____
MONTHLY LATE CHARGE $ _____
ACCRUED LATE CHARGES $ _____ IMPOUND PAYMENTS $ _____

TYPE OF BREACH

_____ NOTE MATURED

_____ DELINQUENT PAYMENTS

_____ DELINQUENT PROPERTY TAXES

_____ FAILURE TO PROVIDE EVIDENCE OF SATISFACTORY FIRE INSURANCE

_____ OTHER

_____ FAILURE TO REPAY THE BENEFICIARY FOR ADVANCES MADE S FOLLOWS:

DATE: __/__/__ AMOUNT $ _____ TO: _____ FOR: _____
DATE: __/__/__ AMOUNT $ _____ TO: _____ FOR: _____
DATE: __/__/__ AMOUNT $ _____ TO: _____ FOR: _____

LAST KNOWN ADDRESS OF CURRENT PROPERTY OWNERS

_____ SAME AS TRUSTORS ON DEED OF TRUST

_____ NEW OWNER(S) ADDRESS (ES)

2. NOTICE OF DEFAULT (NOD)

Notice of Default - continued

Name of Beneficiary or Mortgagee:
Mailing Address
Telephone No.

If you have any questions, you should contact a lawyer or the governmental agency which may have insured your loan.

Notwithstanding the fact that your property is in foreclosure, you may offer your property for sale, provided the sale is concluded prior to the conclusion of the foreclosure.

Remember, **YOU MAY LOSE LEGAL RIGHTS IF YOU DO NOT TAKE PROMPT ACTION** .

NOTICE OF DEFAULT

NOTICE IS HEREBY GIVEN: That Network Foreclosure Services, is duly appointed Trustee under a Deed of Trust dated   , executed by   , as Trustor, in favor of

as Beneficiary, recorded , as Instrument No.   Official Records in the Office of the County Recorder of   , California, describing the land therein:

SEE EXHIBIT 'A' ATTACHED HERETO AND MADE A PART HEREOF.

; that the beneficial interest under
undersigned; that a breach of,
d in that payment has not been

d of Trust, has executed and
d Demand for Sale, and has
evidencing obligations secured
mediately due and payable and
satisfy the obligations secured

RECORDING REQUESTED BY

Network Foreclosure Services

AND WHEN RECORDED MAIL DOCUMENT AND TAX STATEMENT TO:

Network Foreclosure Services
390 Diablo Road, Suite 130
Danville, CA 94526

SPACE ABOVE THIS LINE FOR RECORDER'S USE ONLY

APN:

Trustee's No.:   Loan No.:

NOTICE OF DEFAULT

IMPORTANT NOTICE

IF YOUR PROPERTY IS IN FORECLOSURE BECAUSE YOU ARE BEHIND IN YOUR PAYMENTS, IT MAY BE SOLD WITHOUT ANY COURT ACTION, and you may have the legal right to bring your account in good standing by paying all of your past due payments plus permitted costs and expenses within the time permitted by law for reinstatement of your account, which is normally five business days prior to the date set for the sale of your property. No sale date may be set until three months from the date this Notice of Default may be recorded (which date of recordation appears on this notice). This amount is $ as of   and will increase until your account becomes current.

While your property is in foreclosure, you still must pay other obligations (such as insurance and taxes) required by your note and deed of trust or mortgage. If you fail to make future payments on the loan, pay taxes on the property, provide insurance on the property, or pay other obligations as required in the note and deed of trust or mortgage, the beneficiary or mortgagee may insist that you do so in order to reinstate your account in good standing. In addition, the beneficiary or mortgagee may require as a condition to reinstatement that you provide reliable written evidence that you paid all senior liens, property taxes, and hazard insurance premiums.

Upon your written request, the beneficiary or mortgagee will give you a written itemization of the entire amount you must pay. You may not have to pay the entire unpaid portion of your account, even though full payment was demanded, but you must pay all amounts in default at the time payment is made. However, you and your beneficiary or mortgagee may mutually agree in writing prior to the time the Notice of Sale is posted (which may not be earlier than the end of the three-month period stated above) to, among other things, (1) provide additional time in which to cure the default by transfer of the property or otherwise; or (2) establish a schedule of payments in order to cure your default; or both (1) and (2).

Following the expiration of the time period referred to in the first paragraph of this notice, unless the obligation being foreclosed upon or a separate written agreement between you and your creditor permits a longer period, you have only the legal right to stop the sale of your property by paying the entire amount demanded by your creditor.

To find out the amount you must pay, or to arrange for payment to stop the foreclosure, or if your property is in foreclosure for any other reason, contact:

Page 1 of 2

3. BENEFICIARY TRANSMITTAL LETTER

Network Foreclosure Services
390 Diablo Road, Suite 130
Danville, CA 94526
(925) 831-1250
FAX (925) 314-7969

Month Day, Year

Beneficiary Transmittal Letter

Beneficiary
Contact Person
Address
City, CA Zip Code

Re: Loan #:
   File#:   NFS #
   Comments:

We report as follows in connection with the default we are handling for you (please note items checked):

( )   Enclosed is a copy of the Notice of default. It recorded:

( )   Enclosed is your copy of the Trustee's Sale Guarantee Policy. Please note the following items:

      The Notice of Default recorded on _____ and the three (3) month period prior to publication

      expires on _____. Attached is a Status Report as of ___/___/_____ reflecting

      costs of the Trustee to be recovered should reinstatement occur prior to the expiration

      of the three (3) month period.

( )   We have been informed the Deed of Trust is now in default.

( )   There is a forbearance agreement on this file. We shall hold the file open until further notice.

( )   New bankruptcy filing on this file:

( )   **Please sign the enclosed Substitution of Trustee form in the presence of a Notary and return it to this office together with your original NOTE and DEED OF TRUST as soon as possible. WE CANNOT GO TO PUBLICATION WITHOUT ORIGINAL DOCUMENTS.**

( )   Other: **NOTICE OF SALE, NON-MILITARY AFFIDAVIT, STATUS REPORT, AND BID INSTRUCTIONS.**

      Please call our office to confirm Trustee's fees and costs before accepting reinstatement.

By: _____
    Ken Beasley, Foreclosure Officer
    Network Foreclosure Services, Trustee

4. NOTICE OF TRUSTEE SALE

NOTICE OF TRUSTEE'S SALE UNDER DEED OF TRUST

Loan :   Other: File: NFS #
Investor Loan #   APN #

Said sale will be made, but without covenant or warranty, express or implied regarding title, possession or encumbrances, to satisfy the indebtedness secured by said Deed, advances thereunder, with interest as provided therein, and the unpaid principal balance of the Note secured by said Deed with interest thereon as provided in said Note, fees, charges and expenses of the trustee and the trusts created by said Deed of Trust.

DATED:

Network Foreclosure Services, as said Trustee
390 Diablo Road, Suite 130
Danville, CA 94526
(925) 831-1250

RECORDING REQUESTED BY

WHEN RECORDED MAIL TO:

Network Foreclosure Services
390 Diablo Road, Suite 130
Danville, CA 94526

Loan :   Other: File: NFS #
Investor Loan #   APN #

NOTICE OF TRUSTEE'S SALE UNDER DEED OF TRUST

**YOU ARE IN DEFAULT UNDER A DEED OF TRUST, DATED _____ ,
UNLESS YOU TAKE ACTION TO PROTECT YOUR PROPERTY, IT MAY BE SOLD
AT A PUBLIC SALE. IF YOU NEED AN EXPLANATION OF THE NATURE OF THE
PROCEEDING AGAINST YOU, YOU SHOULD CONTACT A LAWYER.**

NOTICE is hereby given that Network Foreclosure Services, as trustee, or successor trustee, or substituted trustee pursuant to the Deed of trust executed by (OWNER'S NAME).

Recorded on __/__/__ as Instrument No. _____ in Book---, Page---, of Official records in the office of the County Recorder of _____ County, California, and pursuant to the Notice of Default and Election to Sell thereunder recorded __/__/__ in Book---, Page---, as Instrument No. _____ of said Official Records, WILL SELL on __/__/__ at **THE COURT STREET ENTRANCE TO THE COUNTY COURTHOUSE, 123 COURT STREET, (CORNER OF MAIN AND COURT STREET), CITY, CA at 1:30 pm**. AT PUBLIC AUCTION TO THE HIGHEST BIDDER FOR CASH (payable at the time of sale in lawful money of the United States), all right, title and interest conveyed to and now held by it under said Deed of Trust in the property situated in said County and State hereinafter described: As more fully described on said Deed of Trust.

The property address and other common designation, if any, of the real property described above is purported to be:
ADDRESS, CITY, CA ZIP CODE

The undersigned Trustee disclaims any liability for any incorrectness of the property address and other common designation, if any, shown herein.

The total amount of the unpaid balance of the obligation secured by the property to be sold and reasonable estimated costs, expenses and advances at the time of the initial publication of the Note of Sale is: $

In addition to cash, the Trustee will accept a cashier's check drawn on a state or national bank, a check drawn by a state or federal credit union or a check drawn by a state or federal savings and loan association, savings association or savings bank specified in Section 5102 of the Financial Code and authorized to do business in this state. In the event tender other than cash is accepted the Trustee may withhold the issuance of the Trustee's Deed until funds become available to the payee or endorsed as a matter of right.

Page 1

5. TRUSTEE'S DEED UPON SALE

TRUSTEES DEED UPON SALE

Loan :   Other: File: NFS #
Investor Loan #   APN #

    Notice of Trustee's Sale was published once a week for three consecutive weeks commencing ___/___/___ in (enter name of newspaper) , a newspaper, and at least 20 days before the date fixed therein for sale a copy of the Notice of Trustee's Sale was posted in a conspicuous place on the property described above and in one public place in the city where the sale was to be held. At the time and place fixed in said notice, Trustee did, by public announcement, and in said provided, postpone the sale from time to time thereafter and did sell the property described above on ___/___/___ at public auction to the Grantee herein, Grantee being the highest qualified bidder therefore, for $ _____ cash, lawful money of the United States, or by the satisfaction of the indebtedness then secured by said Deed of Trust.

    In WITNESS WHEREOF, NETWORK FORECLOSURE SERVICES, as the Trustee, has this day, ___/___/___ caused its name to be hereunto affixed by its officer thereunto duly authorized by its Corporation By-Laws.

Network Foreclosure Services, as said Trustee

RECORDING REQUESTED BY

WHEN RECORDED MAIL TO:

New Owner
Owner's Address
City, CA Zip Code

Loan :   Other: File: NFS #
Investor Loan #   APN #

TRUSTEES DEED UPON SALE

DOCUMENTARY TRANSFER TAX IS COMPUTED ON FULL VALUE LESS LIENS AND
ENCUMBRANCES REMAINING AT TIME OF SALE $0.00
AMOUNT OF CONSIDERATION $ Final Purchase Amount
AMOUNT OF UNPAID DEBT $ Amount of Total Debt
GRANTEE IS IDENTIFIED AS THE BENEFICIARY.

_____
Declarant's Signature or Agent Determining Tax

Network Foreclosure Services _____
_____
Declarant's Name

    NETWORK FORECLOSURE SERVICES, Trustee, (whereas so designated in the Deed of Trust herein under more particularly described or as duly appointed Trustee), does hereby GRANT and CONVEY to NEW OWNER (herein called Grantee), but without covenant or warranty, express or implied, all right, title and interest conveyed to and now held by it as Trustee under the Deed of Trust in and to the property situated in the City of   , County of   , State of California, described as follows:

(ENTER LEGAL DESCRIPTION)

APN #

    This conveyance is made in compliance with the terms and provisions of the Deed of Trust executed by (HOME OWNER) and recorded ___/___/___, in Book--, Page--, Instrument No. of Official records, in the office of the Recorder of   County, California, under the authority and powers vested in the Trustee designated in the Deed of Trust or as duly appointed Trustee, default having occurred under the Deed of Trust and pursuant to the Notice of Default and Election to Sell under the Deed of Trust recorded ___/___/___, in Book--, Page--, Instrument No.   of Official records. Trustee having complied with all applicable statutory requirements of the State of California and performed all duties required by the Deed of Trust including sending of a Notice of Default and Election to Sell within 10 days after its recording and a Notice of Sale at least 20 days prior to the Sale Date by certified mail, postage pre-paid to each person entitled to notice in compliance with California Civil Code 2924b.

* Mail tax bill to the above

CHAPTER ELEVEN

BANKRUPTCY

Whereas, the foreclosure laws are from state-to-state the bankruptcy laws are Federal. Bankruptcy is available to all people, corporations, and other entities. The laws of bankruptcy have always favored the debtor versus the creditor. A few years ago, the government passed laws to tighten up the requirements to qualify for a bankruptcy and put limits on which dreditors can be wiped out due to the process.

Secured and unsecured creditors have certain rights. The debtor must follow the rules, accurately list all monies owed, and must be honest with their intent. The debtor cannot sell his/her property to avoid listing it as an asset within a certain time period of the bankruptcy filing.

The bankruptcy procedure falls under national law versus a state-to-state rule. Bankruptcy allows a person or corporation, etc., with debt to follow certain procedures that can relieve debt or re-arrange debt.

The main concern in a bankruptcy is that the entity declaring bankruptcy is following the rules, not violating the law, and has the right intent as to why they need to seek relief.

Remember whether you are filing a Chapter 7, 11, or a 13, your intent and the reason why you are filing must be taken into consideration. Unfortunately most people look at bankruptcy as a tool to get rid of debt and start a new life. That could be okay if done in the right way.

Over the past twenty years, I have been involved in many cases where a person who owed obligations to creditors either got tired of paying, or felt that they had no alternative but to seek relief. Declaring bankruptcy has pros and cons. Once a debtor has filed bankruptcy he/she will have ruined their credit and will need to re-establish their portfolio over a five to seven year time period. The debtor will get rid of some debt, but the stigma will follow them for many years.

When I represent an investor who has made a loan to a person under legal terms and the borrower stops paying his/her obligation it is my duty to find out how the investor can be protected.

Whether a debtor files a Chapter 7, 11, or 13, it is imperative that the creditor be aggressive when going after an obligation that is owed to them. I have gone into bankruptcy court many times and filed a dismissal of a bankruptcy so that I could continue a foreclosure that was stopped by the action. If a debtor cannot show a valid reason why they can hold onto a property, a financial commitment is made to show how a payment plan is to be structured. If a plan is established the trustee might consider dismissing the bankruptcy (applies to Chapter 11 and 13).

Many people file bankruptcy for the right reasons, medical bills, financial disaster, and even the current economy with all the sub-prime loans — and I feel that you always have the right to protect yourself against loss. Remember if you can work things out and can present a plan that will solve your problems then you should always seek any avenue available to make things better for yourself.

Under Chapter 13, for individuals, and Chapter 11, for entities (corporations, LLCs, partnerships), the debtor has a right to file a plan, show the trustee that they can perform, and set up a payment schedule that will work for not only the debtor, but the creditor as well. The only time a creditor should challenge the plan is if they feel that the filing of the bankruptcy was done unjustly and will only protect the assets of the debtor. A creditor would rather have the entity that owes them the obligation live up to the commitment, instead of having to take back a property through foreclosure.

Under the Chapter 7 bankruptcy the debtor is basically liquidating their investment subject to their homeowner exemption. The creditor either needs to get a release of their obligation from the courts or get a dismissal to continue with his/her foreclosure to take back a property. In today's economy does the creditor really want to take back the property and try to recoup their investment? Chapter 7 bankruptcy has a built-in exemption for a personal residence, stating that you cannot force a debtor to sell a property unless he/she is unable to make arrangements to pay the monthly payments on the property.

Whether you are a debtor or creditor always seek legal advice from a bankruptcy attorney to evaluate your position, understand your position and determine if you have an exit plan that can solve the immediate problem.

When someone owes you money especially in today's market their threat to go into bankruptcy if you do not forgive late payments or re-write their debt, is probably real!

What are the different types of Bankruptcies?

Chapter 7, Chapter 11, and Chapter 13 are the three types that I'll discuss here. There are more, but they will not affect the average individual, or private entity.

What is the person who files the Bankruptcy?

The person who needs bankruptcy relief is called the debtor.

Who is the person, or entity, that is owed the money?

The person, or entity, that is owed the money is called the creditor.

Why would a person, or entity, file Bankruptcy?

The reasons for bankruptcy vary from individuals to corporations. Examples of reasons are:
- Illness and large medical bills
- Foreclosure of primary residence
- Job layoff and mounting bills
- A lawsuit that threatens to attach all of your assets

What is a Chapter 7 Bankruptcy?

A Chapter 7 bankruptcy is a court order releasing a debtor from all of his/her dischargeable debts. This form of bankruptcy permits the debtor to discharge certain debts by filing a case in the bankruptcy court. Not all debts will get discharged. All bankruptcies will stop a foreclosure for a time period.

Who may file a Chapter 7 Bankruptcy?

Any person who resides, does business in, or has property in the United States may file a Chapter 7 bankruptcy.

The one exemption is any person who has been involved in another bankruptcy case that was dismissed within the last 180 days on certain grounds. There is a specific time period that you must wait once a bankruptcy is dismissed or closed, before you can file again.

Where do I file a Bankruptcy action?

You must file in the bankruptcy court in the district where your principal business or residence has been for the past 180-days.

Does a Chapter 7 Bankruptcy affect a lawsuit or attachment?

A debtor may retain certain personal and household items and they may retain exempt status property that is subject only to a judgment lien without paying the creditor anything (e.g., personal residence, personal property and an automobile).

How long does a Chapter 7 Bankruptcy last?

A Chapter 7 bankruptcy begins with the filing of the case and ends with the closing of the case by the courts. The estimated time for the bankruptcy is three to four months to discharge.

What is the filing fee for a Chapter 7 Bankruptcy?

Filing fees range from $250 to $400. If you use a bankruptcy attorney it will be more costly.

What is a Chapter 11 Bankruptcy?

A Chapter 11 (Reorganization of Debt) permits a business to obtain protection from its creditors, while it attempts to reorganize or liquidate itself. Chapter 11 can also be filed by an individual.

Who May file a Chapter 11 Bankruptcy?

Anyone may file who doesn't fall into the following:

- Government Agency
- Estate
- Non-Business Trust
- Stockbroker
- Insurance Company
- Bank

Who is allowed to file a Chapter 11 Bankruptcy?

Any of the following:

- Large Business
- Small Business
- Corporation
- LLC
- Partnership
- Sole Proprietor

Is there a third party named in a Chapter 11 Bankruptcy to monitor and oversee the procedures?

The Chapter 11 bankruptcy appoints a trustee whose function is to monitor the case and appoint one or more creditor committees. The Trustee presides at meetings with the creditors.

What does the reorganization consist of in a Chapter 11 Bankruptcy?

After looking at what the creditors present the trustee can either extend the time for repayment of debt, restructure the business plan or decline certain parts of the plan.

In the Chapter 11 Bankruptcy what are the usual time periods?

The usual time periods are separated into two phases:

Phase I – Lasts six to eight months

Phase II – Lasts three to five years if needed

What is the "Plan" presented to the Court under Chapter 11 Bankruptcy Reorganization?

A Chapter 11 plan must be confirmed by the bankruptcy court. The judge signs an order approving the plan and a ruling that the debtor and all creditors and interest holders are bound to by the provisions of the plan. The debtor must file his/her plan during the first 120-days and the debtor must get the acceptance of the plan by the creditors within 180-days after the case has been filed.

What is a Chapter 13 Bankruptcy?

The Chapter 13 (Adjustment of Debt) bankruptcy permits an individual to repay all or of his/her debt under the supervision and protection of the bankruptcy court.

What goes into the "Debtor's Plan" when you file under Chapter 13 Bankruptcy?

A debtor's plan is filed to structure the repayment of all or a portion of a person's debt to the court and the court must approve the plan. The Chapter 13 trustee collects the money paid in by the debtor and disburses it to the creditors as set forth in the debtor's plan.

What is the Debtor able to keep under the Chapter 13 Plan?

Under the Chapter 13 plan, the debtor is usually permitted to keep his/her non-exempt property and is required to pay off as much debt as possible. The debtor is then released from liability for the balance of his/her debt.

What is the emphasis of the Chapter 13 Bankruptcy Plan?

The Chapter 13 bankruptcy plan is the adjustment of debt. The written plan that is presented to the Court by the Debtor shows how the debts are to be paid.

Who is the Trustee in the Chapter 13 Bankruptcy?

The trustee is an officer of the court who collects payments from the debtor on how the debts have agreed to be paid.

What is the time period for a Chapter 13 Bankruptcy if accepted?

Chapter 13 bankruptcy must last three years unless all debts can be paid off in full before that time period. This plan can be bought out early if everyone agrees.

Who can file the Chapter 13 bankruptcy plan?

Any person who does the following:

- Resides or does business in the United States
- Has a regular income
- Has unsecured debts of less than $307,675.00
- Has secured debts of less than $922,975.00

Where to file a Chapter 13 Bankruptcy?

The Chapter 13 will be filed in the bankruptcy court that is a unit of the Federal District Court.

Can you convert a Chapter 7 to a Chapter 13, or a Chapter 13 to a Chapter 7, during the course of the Bankruptcy?

Yes. As long as the court "okays" the transfer and the other chapter is dismissed in the right way.

What is the filing fee for a Chapter 13 Bankruptcy?

The range is between $500 and $1000 unless you have obtained the services of a bankruptcy attorney.

Do all Bankruptcy filings automatically stop a Foreclosure that has been started on a Trustor who is also the Debtor on the Bankruptcy?

Yes. The bankruptcy filing automatically stops or freezes the foreclosure. However, the beneficiary can hire an attorney to represent them to have his/her deed of trust released from the bankruptcy so that they can continue the foreclosure.

BANKRUPTCY SAMPLE DOCUMENTS:

1. FORM TO FILE A CHAPTER 7, CHAPTER 11, OR CHAPTER 13 BANKRUPTCY (PAGE 1 OF 3)

B 1 (Official Form 1) (1/08)

United States Bankruptcy Court	Voluntary Petition

Name of Debtor (if individual, enter Last, First, Middle):	Name of Joint Debtor (Spouse) (Last, First, Middle):
All Other Names used by the Debtor in the last 8 years (include married, maiden, and trade names):	All Other Names used by the Joint Debtor in the last 8 years (include married, maiden, and trade names):
Last four digits of Soc. Sec. or Individual-Taxpayer I.D. (ITIN) No./Complete EIN (if more than one, state all):	Last four digits of Soc. Sec. or Individual-Taxpayer I.D. (ITIN) No./Complete EIN (if more than one, state all):
Street Address of Debtor (No. and Street, City, and State): ZIP CODE	Street Address of Joint Debtor (No. and Street, City, and State): ZIP CODE
County of Residence or of the Principal Place of Business:	County of Residence or of the Principal Place of Business:
Mailing Address of Debtor (if different from street address): ZIP CODE	Mailing Address of Joint Debtor (if different from street address): ZIP CODE
Location of Principal Assets of Business Debtor (if different from street address above): ZIP CODE	

Type of Debtor
(Form of Organization)
(Check one box.)

- ☐ Individual (includes Joint Debtors) *See Exhibit D on page 2 of this form.*
- ☐ Corporation (includes LLC and LLP)
- ☐ Partnership
- ☐ Other (If debtor is not one of the above entities, check this box and state type of entity below.)

Nature of Business
(Check one box.)

- ☐ Health Care Business
- ☐ Single Asset Real Estate as defined in 11 U.S.C. § 101(51B)
- ☐ Railroad
- ☐ Stockbroker
- ☐ Commodity Broker
- ☐ Clearing Bank
- ☐ Other

Tax-Exempt Entity
(Check box, if applicable.)

- ☐ Debtor is a tax-exempt organization under Title 26 of the United States Code (the Internal Revenue Code).

Chapter of Bankruptcy Code Under Which the Petition is Filed (Check one box.)

- ☐ Chapter 7
- ☐ Chapter 9
- ☐ Chapter 11
- ☐ Chapter 12
- ☐ Chapter 13
- ☐ Chapter 15 Petition for Recognition of a Foreign Main Proceeding
- ☐ Chapter 15 Petition for Recognition of a Foreign Nonmain Proceeding

Nature of Debts
(Check one box.)

- ☐ Debts are primarily consumer debts, defined in 11 U.S.C. § 101(8) as "incurred by an individual primarily for a personal, family, or household purpose."
- ☐ Debts are primarily business debts.

Filing Fee (Check one box.)

- ☐ Full Filing Fee attached.
- ☐ Filing Fee to be paid in installments (applicable to individuals only). Must attach signed application for the court's consideration certifying that the debtor is unable to pay fee except in installments. Rule 1006(b). See Official Form 3A.
- ☐ Filing Fee waiver requested (applicable to chapter 7 individuals only). Must attach signed application for the court's consideration. See Official Form 3B.

Chapter 11 Debtors

Check one box:
- ☐ Debtor is a small business debtor as defined in 11 U.S.C. § 101(51D).
- ☐ Debtor is not a small business debtor as defined in 11 U.S.C. § 101(51D).

Check if:
- ☐ Debtor's aggregate noncontingent liquidated debts (excluding debts owed to insiders or affiliates) are less than $2,190,000.

Check all applicable boxes:
- ☐ A plan is being filed with this petition.
- ☐ Acceptances of the plan were solicited prepetition from one or more classes of creditors, in accordance with 11 U.S.C. § 1126(b).

Statistical/Administrative Information

- ☐ Debtor estimates that funds will be available for distribution to unsecured creditors.
- ☐ Debtor estimates that, after any exempt property is excluded and administrative expenses paid, there will be no funds available for distribution to unsecured creditors.

THIS SPACE IS FOR COURT USE ONLY

Estimated Number of Creditors

☐ 1-49	☐ 50-99	☐ 100-199	☐ 200-999	☐ 1,000-5,000	☐ 5,001-10,000	☐ 10,001-25,000	☐ 25,001-50,000	☐ 50,000-100,000	☐ Over 100,000

Estimated Assets

☐ $0 to $50,000	☐ $50,001 to $100,000	☐ $100,001 to $500,000	☐ $500,001 to $1 million	☐ $1,000,001 to $10 million	☐ $10,000,001 to $50 million	☐ $50,000,001 to $100 million	☐ $100,000,001 to $500 million	☐ $500,000,001 to $1 billion	☐ More than $1 billion

Estimated Liabilities

☐ $0 to $50,000	☐ $50,001 to $100,000	☐ $100,001 to $500,000	☐ $500,001 to $1 million	☐ $1,000,001 to $10 million	☐ $10,000,001 to $50 million	☐ $50,000,001 to $100 million	☐ $100,000,001 to $500 million	☐ $500,000,001 to $1 billion	☐ More than $1 billion

FORM TO FILE A CHAPTER 7, CHAPTER 11, OR CHAPTER 13 BANKRUPTCY (PAGE 2 OF 3)

B 1 (Official Form 1) (1/08)   Page 2

Voluntary Petition *(This page must be completed and filed in every case.)*	Name of Debtor(s):	

All Prior Bankruptcy Cases Filed Within Last 8 Years (If more than two, attach additional sheet.)		
Location Where Filed:	Case Number:	Date Filed:
Location Where Filed:	Case Number:	Date Filed:

Pending Bankruptcy Case Filed by any Spouse, Partner, or Affiliate of this Debtor (If more than one, attach additional sheet.)		
Name of Debtor:	Case Number:	Date Filed:
District:	Relationship:	Judge:

Exhibit A	**Exhibit B**
(To be completed if debtor is required to file periodic reports (e.g., forms 10K and 10Q) with the Securities and Exchange Commission pursuant to Section 13 or 15(d) of the Securities Exchange Act of 1934 and is requesting relief under chapter 11.)	(To be completed if debtor is an individual whose debts are primarily consumer debts.) I, the attorney for the petitioner named in the foregoing petition, declare that I have informed the petitioner that [he or she] may proceed under 7, 11, 12, or 13 of title 11, United States Code, and have explained the relief available under each such chapter. I further certify that I have delivered to the debtor the notice required by 11 U.S.C. § 342(b).
☐ Exhibit A is attached and made a part of this petition.	X _____ Signature of Attorney for Debtor(s) (Date)

Exhibit C

Does the debtor own or have possession of any property that poses or is alleged to pose a threat of imminent and identifiable harm to public health or safety?

☐ Yes, and Exhibit C is attached and made a part of this petition.

☐ No.

Exhibit D

(To be completed by every individual debtor. If a joint petition is filed, each spouse must complete and attach a separate Exhibit D.)

  ☐ Exhibit D completed and signed by the debtor is attached and made a part of this petition.

If this is a joint petition:

  ☐ Exhibit D also completed and signed by the joint debtor is attached and made a part of this petition.

Information Regarding the Debtor - Venue
(Check any applicable box.)

  ☐ Debtor has been domiciled or has had a residence, principal place of business, or principal assets in this District for 180 days immediately preceding the date of this petition or for a longer part of such 180 days than in any other District.

  ☐ There is a bankruptcy case concerning debtor's affiliate, general partner, or partnership pending in this District.

  ☐ Debtor is a debtor in a foreign proceeding and has its principal place of business or principal assets in the United States in this District, or has no principal place of business or assets in the United States but is a defendant in an action or proceeding [in a federal or state court] in this District, or the interests of the parties will be served in regard to the relief sought in this District.

Certification by a Debtor Who Resides as a Tenant of Residential Property
(Check all applicable boxes.)

  ☐ Landlord has a judgment against the debtor for possession of debtor's residence. (If box checked, complete the following.)

      _____
      (Name of landlord that obtained judgment)

      _____
      (Address of landlord)

  ☐ Debtor claims that under applicable nonbankruptcy law, there are circumstances under which the debtor would be permitted to cure the entire monetary default that gave rise to the judgment for possession, after the judgment for possession was entered, and

  ☐ Debtor has included with this petition the deposit with the court of any rent that would become due during the 30-day period after the filing of the petition.

  ☐ Debtor certifies that he/she has served the Landlord with this certification. (11 U.S.C. § 362(l)).

FORM TO FILE A CHAPTER 7, CHAPTER 11, OR CHAPTER 13 BANKRUPTCY (PAGE 3 OF 3)

B 1 (Official Form) 1 (1/08)	Page 3
Voluntary Petition *(This page must be completed and filed in every case.)*	Name of Debtor(s):

Signatures

Signature(s) of Debtor(s) (Individual/Joint)	Signature of a Foreign Representative
I declare under penalty of perjury that the information provided in this petition is true and correct. [If petitioner is an individual whose debts are primarily consumer debts and has chosen to file under chapter 7] I am aware that I may proceed under chapter 7, 11, 12 or 13 of title 11, United States Code, understand the relief available under each such chapter, and choose to proceed under chapter 7. [If no attorney represents me and no bankruptcy petition preparer signs the petition] I have obtained and read the notice required by 11 U.S.C. § 342(b). I request relief in accordance with the chapter of title 11, United States Code, specified in this petition.	I declare under penalty of perjury that the information provided in this petition is true and correct, that I am the foreign representative of a debtor in a foreign proceeding, and that I am authorized to file this petition. (Check only one box.) ☐ I request relief in accordance with chapter 15 of title 11, United States Code. Certified copies of the documents required by 11 U.S.C. § 1515 are attached. ☐ Pursuant to 11 U.S.C. § 1511, I request relief in accordance with the chapter of title 11 specified in this petition. A certified copy of the order granting recognition of the foreign main proceeding is attached.
X _____ Signature of Debtor X _____ Signature of Joint Debtor _____ Telephone Number (if not represented by attorney) _____ Date	X _____ (Signature of Foreign Representative) _____ (Printed Name of Foreign Representative) _____ Date
Signature of Attorney*	**Signature of Non-Attorney Bankruptcy Petition Preparer**
X _____ Signature of Attorney for Debtor(s) _____ Printed Name of Attorney for Debtor(s) _____ Firm Name _____ Address _____ Telephone Number _____ Date *In a case in which § 707(b)(4)(D) applies, this signature also constitutes a certification that the attorney has no knowledge after an inquiry that the information in the schedules is incorrect.	I declare under penalty of perjury that: (1) I am a bankruptcy petition preparer as defined in 11 U.S.C. § 110, (2) I prepared this document for compensation and have provided the debtor with a copy of this document and the notices and information required under 11 U.S.C. §§ 110(b), 110(h), and 342(b); and, (3) if rules or guidelines have been promulgated pursuant to 11 U.S.C. § 110(h) setting a maximum fee for services chargeable by bankruptcy petition preparers, I have given the debtor notice of the maximum amount before preparing any document for filing for a debtor or accepting any fee from the debtor, as required in that section. Official Form 19 is attached. _____ Printed Name and title, if any, of Bankruptcy Petition Preparer _____ Social-Security number (If the bankruptcy petition preparer is not an individual, state the Social-Security number of the officer, principal, responsible person or partner of the bankruptcy petition preparer.) (Required by 11 U.S.C. § 110.) _____ Address X _____ _____ Date
Signature of Debtor (Corporation/Partnership)	Signature of bankruptcy petition preparer or officer, principal, responsible person, or partner whose Social-Security number is provided above.
I declare under penalty of perjury that the information provided in this petition is true and correct, and that I have been authorized to file this petition on behalf of the debtor. The debtor requests the relief in accordance with the chapter of title 11, United States Code, specified in this petition. X _____ Signature of Authorized Individual _____ Printed Name of Authorized Individual _____ Title of Authorized Individual _____ Date	Names and Social-Security numbers of all other individuals who prepared or assisted in preparing this document unless the bankruptcy petition preparer is not an individual. If more than one person prepared this document, attach additional sheets conforming to the appropriate official form for each person. *A bankruptcy petition preparer's failure to comply with the provisions of title 11 and the Federal Rules of Bankruptcy Procedure may result in fines or imprisonment or both. 11 U.S.C. § 110; 18 U.S.C. § 156.*

CHAPTER TWELVE

REOS (REAL ESTATE/BANK OWNED PROPERTIES)

The foreclosure process, a topic that has been in the news constantly since 2006, has been covered in a previous chapter. It was noted that by the middle of 2009 over two-million foreclosures will have taken place in the United States. The foreclosure rate in California alone is up 79% over the past few years.

Sub-prime loans have not only affected the consumer but as we are seeing on the news lenders — like Washington Mutual, Wachovia and IndyMac — to name a few have either failed or been taken over. Wall Street seems on the verge of collapsing.

"REOs" are basically "bank owned properties." This occurs when the lender/bank after threatening foreclosure and trying to work with the consumer to possibly do a "short sale" has decided to take the property back.

Once a bank takes a property back they have to be prepared to pay for any damage the borrower has done to the property due to the anger and frustration of losing his/her home. And the bank does not have access to the premises until they have completed the foreclosure process and received a trustee's deed to the property.

Most REOs are assigned to an asset manager who then contacts a realtor in the area to gain access and to determine a "Broker Price Opinion" (BPO) value. Unfortunately, these properties are usually trashed, the yards are ruined, and the swimming pools are green and need repair. REOs are usually sold "AS-IS" with little or no fix-up. The price set by the bank must reflect the condition of the property and the current economy.

The realtor will put the property on the local MLS, put a lock box on the premises, and will usually set the value to attract multiple offers. The price should be "Fair Market Value" but sometimes an REO can be purchased under property value.

Once the listing realtor receives a purchase agreement from a buyer he/she will submit it to the bank's representative for consideration. Unlike a regular purchase agreement which is usually reviewed in two days the REO offer will take three to seven days to get a response. The process is slow and takes time because of the chain of command. When you are buying a property "AS-IS," you still need the due diligence of all the property inspections. If you are representing the buyer make sure the property is not destroyed or in need of major repairs.

When representing the buyer what credits can you ask for? The process depends on how many offers the bank has received, what price you are getting the property for, and finally your emotional attachment to the property as the buyer. My feeling is always ask for as much as you can get. The contingencies you put in your offer are also limited under an REO sale so as a Buyer it is wise to ask for a 15-day loan and appraisal contingency and ten-days for inspections.

Most escrows take thirty to forty days, but the REO escrow will take forty to sixty days due to the lack of direct contact with the seller. A "contingency" is a condition of sale that allows certain time periods to execute your contract. If you do not agree with a contingency then you have a right to break the contract.

In a regular transaction the seller must provide disclosures to the buyer stating the condition of the property. Under the REO sale the disclosures do not exist because the bank did a foreclosure to get the property back. A property inspection by the buyer is crucial to determine whether or not you feel comfortable with purchasing the property. An "AS-IS" purchase means that the seller is not doing any repairs.

Most buyers end up purchasing REOs using an FHA loan, and minimizing the down payment. The REO must be your permanent residence in order for you to be able to qualify for an FHA loan. Most investors end up putting 30% to 40% down so that they can qualify then rent out the property for a positive cash-flow.

Are REOs good investments? That can only be answered after holding onto the property for a reasonable amount of time. Anytime you can purchase real estate under value it can be a good thing.

The trend for foreclosures, short sales, and REOs will probably exist for the next few years. The current market will take some time to fix itself. Lenders will need time to create new programs, new guidelines, and a better system to protect all parties.

Only time will tell if have you have done the right thing by purchasing an REO.

EXAMPLE OF HOW THE REO PROCESS WORKS
by Jason LoGuidice

A client who is an investor approached me and wanted to purchase a bank owned multi-unit building. We spent three months searching for the right property. We found two identical buildings that were next to one another. Both buildings were listed in the low $400,000s and needed a substantial amount of work — but they were still priced competitively. Since this particular Buyer had a family member with an engineering and construction background we were able to put in a low bid based on the scope of work that was needed to improve the condition of the property.

After three counter offers we finally reached an agreement for a purchase price on each building that was almost $100,000 under the original asking price. Luckily the listing broker was very cooperative and helpful in keeping the lines of communication open with the asset manager at the bank. We submitted an offer on June 3, 2008, and went back and forth with counter offers until June 27, 2008.

Once the properties were in escrow everything went smoothly on the buyer's end because the buyer had stellar credit and a large down payment. We were also using a seasoned mortgage broker who was familiar with the ins and outs of an REO purchase. Close of escrow took place about three months from the day we made the first offer.

Another issue to be aware of with bank owned properties is that legally the bank is not required to provide you with disclosures like a seller in a conventional sale is. We did our homework and we had property, pest, home, roof, and foundation inspections to be sure we were well informed on all of the issues with both properties.

Once we did all of our due diligence we were able to remove our contingencies without having to get an extension and move towards signing loan documents. The asset manager was so inundated with sales it was difficult to get the bank representative to sign the loan documents delaying the closing. Long story short, if you are working with a professional who is willing to do the leg work and research and you have a strong mortgage broker you will be able to find good values on Bank Owned properties in this market — it just takes the right combination of expertise, persistence, and patience.

These particular investments will pay off in the long run because even after putting out money on improvements the buyer will still have a positive cash-flow and will be able to sell these properties with a nice profit down the road or hold onto them for a long period of time and realize appreciation and positive cash-flow from the rent.

The end result was the client was happy and felt that he had gotten a good deal on these two REO properties and is now pursuing other REO opportunities.

POTENTIAL PROBLEMS TO BE AWARE OF WHEN DOING AN REO PURCHASE

1. Banks are not required to provide disclosures.

2. The time period between the submission of documents to the execution is generally three to five business days.

3. Several people are involved in the transaction — usually the broker/agent is very busy so you are dealing with an assistant — and everything must go from the buyer to the agent…to the seller's agent…to asset manager…to a longer chain of command.

4. Contingencies are passive meaning that if you don't object to the removal of a contingency in writing the bank will consider it "removed" unlike in a conventional sale.

5. Banks are likely to shorten the contingency time periods to fifteen-days for the loan contingency and ten-days for inspections, from the usual seventeen-days on a regular sale.

6. Banks rewrite their own contracts so you must take extra care to look for additional stipulations.

7. There is room for negotiation but nine out of ten times the bank picks the escrow company (in California, it's almost always First American Title).

8. In some cases the listing will state that the seller (bank) will not give any credits for closing costs.

9. REO properties are competitively priced based on a few BPOs (Broker Price Opinions).

CHAPTER THIRTEEN

THE 1031 EXCHANGE

One of the few remaining avenues through which investors can build wealth without the burden of paying taxes is the use of a tax-deferred exchange. If I could show you a perfectly legal way to pyramid your wealth into a larger net-worth – without paying taxes – would you be interested?

The nice thing about the 1031 Tax Exchange is that everyone who owns investment property can benefit from it. Every year thousands of knowledgeable taxpayers use the tax-deferred exchange to dispose of one investment property to acquire a more desirable property or properties—and this transfer is done at a tax savings.

The benefit of deferring taxes on real estate has been around for years but since the 1986 Tax Reform Act more investors have taken advantage of using the Internal Revenue Code §1031 in the sale of real estate investment property. The 1993 Clinton tax bill did not affect the benefits of doing exchanges but each year bills are introduced that might eventually change the direction of the 1031 Tax Exchange. In 1997, a new "Capital Gains" law was passed that increased the number of exemptions for a personal residence.

The questions and answers asked in this chapter will give you the basis to better understand 1031 Tax Exchanges. We are not dealing with defined issues in regard to the rules that regulate exchanges. The Internal Revenue Service has regulations that structure the 1031. They also rely on the intent of the taxpayer, the intent of the property, and the structure of the transaction.

People, primarily do exchanges to avoid taxes that erode the equity they've earned in their investment property. Remember — personal property does not qualify for an investor exchange — and the exchanged property must be held for investment purposes only (intent).

The 1031 Tax Exchange has taken a different path over the past twenty years. Prior to the judicial decisions made in 1979 and 1984 all exchanges had to be simultaneous. The difficulties in arranging for a series of properties to close escrow at the same time were onerous. Since the non-simultaneous exchange (Starker) case of 1979 investors have been allowed a period of time between the sale of one investment property and the purchase of another— and have enjoyed the benefits of more exchange options.

The reverse exchange was finally approved by the Internal Revenue Service allowing the exchanger to buy a replacement property (new) before selling the relinquished (exchange) property. Use of a construction (improvement) exchange is beneficial to builders who want to take advantage of the tax benefits and build a replacement property to qualify for an exchange.

After reading this Chapter, and understanding the different ways an Investor can sell his/her Investment Property—and save tax dollars—you will understand the concept, and many benefits, of "EXCHANGING."

TYPES OF EXCHANGES

The first question we must ask, and understand, is the obvious...

What is an Exchange?

An exchange is the sale of one or more properties held for productive use in a trade or business, or for further investment. The seller/exchanger must acquire other investment property or properties resulting in one continuous investment.

What are the requirements of an Exchange?

The Internal Revenue Service usually looks at the intent of the transaction, the qualification of the property being sold, the replacement property(ies) and whether all of the rules under Internal Revenue Code (IRC) 1031 are being followed.

Why would a Seller want to do an Exchange?

The main reason a property owner would consider doing a 1031 Tax Exchange on his/her investment property would be to save on income taxes. The property owner must also examine the possibility that by doing an exchange he/she could be diversifying his/her property holdings, increasing his/her depreciable basis, and possibly causing the property in question to be easier to market.

What do the numbers "1031" mean?

"1031" refers to the IRS Tax Code and its referral to "investment property" transactions.

Is there more than one type of 1031 Tax Exchange?

Yes, there are.

What is the most commonly used 1031 Tax Exchange?

The non-simultaneous (delayed) exchange is most common. This form of exchange was made famous by the 1984 court case known as the "Starker Exchange."

What are the procedures that take place in doing a Non-Simultaneous (Delayed) Exchange?

The non-simultaneous exchange has the following criteria:
- Close sale of exchange property
- Intermediary holds exchange proceeds
- 45-days to target replacement properties
- 180-days to close escrow on all replacement properties

When I sell my personal residence, what IRS Tax Code does this fall under?

This is called a "1034 Tax Exchange."

What is it called when legislation allows for cities, counties, and governments to exercise their option to take over private property for their specific use?

This is called a "1033 Exchange," or "involuntary exchange."

Why have I heard the phrase "1031 Tax Exchange" more often over the past ten years?

The Tax Reform Act of 1986 has made the tax-deferred exchange a preferable alternative to the taxable sale.

What did the 1986 Tax Reform Act cover?

The 1986 Tax Reform Act passed laws that:

- Minimized the preferential treatment of "capital gains," resulting in larger tax payments from the sale of real estate
- Gave a longer recovery period for depreciation of investment property resulting in reduced depreciation deductions
- Affected the passive loss rule possibly reducing or eliminating this type of tax shelter

What are the different types of a 1031 Tax Exchanges used in the Real estate market?

The following exchanges are used in connection with the sale of an investment property. (Note: There are different types of exchanges and in the eyes of the IRS some of these procedures could be questioned):

- Simultaneous exchange
- Non-simultaneous (delayed) exchange
- Reverse exchange
- Construction (improvement) exchange

What is Simultaneous Exchange?

This type of exchange occurs when both the sale of the investment property and the purchase of the replacement property close at the same time.

When I do a Simultaneous Exchange do I need to use a Facilitator/Intermediary to coordinate my Exchange?

No. As long as you can get the buyer of the property you are selling and/or the seller of the property you are purchasing to act as the so-called "strawman."

Is there liability to either the Buyer or Seller of my Exchange transaction, acting as the Facilitator?

Yes. There is a possibility that by either the buyer or seller acting as the intermediary for your exchange they may open themselves up to a lawsuit for any claims from environmental agencies.

In a Simultaneous Exchange do the Exchanger's proceeds ever leave the escrow?

No. The escrow agent transfers the sale proceeds to the replacement property escrow and closes with the exchange funds.

What is the most popular type of Exchange used by Investors?

The non-simultaneous (delayed) exchange is the most popular type of exchange. The reason for its popularity is that it allows the exchanger time to sell his/her relinquished property, time to target replacement property(ies), and time to coordinate the close of escrow.

If I do a 1031 Tax-Deferred Exchange, is there a time period for me to follow, in regard to identification, and the close of escrow, on my Replacement Property(ies)?

The identification period begins upon the transfer of the relinquished property, and ends forty-five days thereafter. The Exchange period begins on the date of the transfer of the relinquished property and ends 180-days thereafter or on the due date (including extensions) of the taxpayer's return.

Upon the close of my Relinquished Property, in a Non-Simultaneous Exchange, can I keep my proceeds in an account set up by me—or does a third party have to hold the funds?

Under the 1031 Tax Code the sales proceeds that will be used for the exchange must be held in a qualified account controlled by the intermediary.

How does the Exchanger identify his/her Replacement Property or properties to the Intermediary?

The replacement property must be designated in a written document, signed by the taxpayer and hand delivered, mailed, or faxed to the Intermediary on or before the last day of the 45-day identification period.

What information is the Exchanger required to put in the identification letter?

The exchanger must be able to identify all properties being targeted, in one of the following ways:

- Street address

- Legal description

- Assessors Parcel Number (APN)

How many properties can the Exchanger identify (target) within the 45-day time period on a Delayed Exchange?

There are three "property rules" that must be followed when targeting replacement property(ies). The number of properties that can be listed will depend on which of these three rules you follow.

What are the three "Property Identification Rules"?

The three "property identification rules" are as follows:

1. There is no limit to the three property values.
2. The "200% Rule" that states that you can list any number of properties, as long as their aggregate fair market value as of the

end of the identification period does not exceed 200% of all relinquished property on the date the relinquished property was transferred by the exchanger.

3. The "95% Rule" that allows any number of replacement properties identified before the end of the identification period and received before the end of the identification period. The exchanger must acquire a value which is at least 95% of the aggregate fair market value of all identified replacement property(ies).

If I present my target Replacement Property to the Intermediary before the 45-day period can I add new Replacement Properties after the designated time period?

No. The exchanger must stay with the target properties presented to the intermediary within the time period. If the exchanger fails to complete the exchange within the necessary time period the exchange will be deemed void.

Can I add a new target property(ies) to my list and present it to the Intermediary before the 45-day period if I feel that one of the properties on my list will not qualify?

Yes. New properties can be added until midnight of the 45th-day.

What is considered a target or Replacement Property(s)?

The basis of the replacement property is the basis of the relinquished property decreased by the amount of money received increased by any money given and increased by any gain or decreased by any loss recognized by the exchanger.

What happens if I cannot complete the purchase of my replacement property(ies) before the expiration of the 180-day period?

The exchange will be void if not completed in the required 180-day time period. The exchange period starts the day the relinquished property is transferred and no extension time will be added to the time period whether it is a weekend, holiday, or circumstance due to natural causes.

If I have 180-days to complete my Exchange what happens if I file my tax returns for the year of the Exchange, before the Exchange time period expires?

Example: If I sell my property in October, 2005 normally I would have until April 15, 2006 to file my returns.

You should consult your accountant when filing your return if your exchange straddles two tax years and there is a delay in filing one return until the exchange is complete. The exchanger can extend his/her April 15 filing deadline to give them the maximum 180-day period to close.

I have heard that some Investors find properties to purchase before they are able to sell their Exchange property. Can they do an Exchange this way?

This is called a reverse exchange. The IRS has finally accepted this form of exchange. The exchanger must find an intermediary to purchase the "up-leg" (replacement) property and hold it until the exchanger can sell his/her "down-leg" (relinquished) property. The intermediary serves as the holding party in this type of transaction.

Is the Reverse Exchange used that much by Investors?

Yes. More and more investors find property they would like to purchase but because his/her exchange property is in an area where sales are soft, they cannot do a regular exchange. To save on paying taxes they must look at alternatives that will allow them to repurchase property and receive tax benefits.

If the Investor/Exchanger does a Reverse Exchange, who is responsible for maintenance of the property, being held, while the transaction is being completed?

The exchanger takes care of the property management, payments, repairs, and insurance and protects the Intermediary as to any liability, while the replacement property is being held.

I have heard that the Exchanger can target vacant land, then use some of the Exchange proceeds to improve the property. Is this true?

This is partially true. This type of exchange is called an improvement or construction exchange. The exchanger cannot purchase the land in his/her name but must use a holding company, builder, or intermediary to facilitate the transaction.

Is the Construction Exchange a valid tool to an Investor, when acquiring his/ her Replacement Property?

The construction exchange is very valuable. With certain restrictions, it allows the exchanger to save tax dollars, build something they really desire, and target new construction.

If an Exchanger wants to do a Construction (Improvement) Exchange, must he/she identify the improvements to be made?

When the exchanger targets replacement property that is vacant land, the improvements, or new construction, must be described with as much detail as is practical.

With a Construction Exchange, can the Exchanger be on title while the improvements are being made?

No. The exchanger cannot be on title while the improvements are being made. Work done with the exchange proceeds must be completed, and the money spent, before the exchanger goes on title. The intermediary or holding company must own the property while it is being improved.

Can the Exchanger control the property during the construction phase of the Exchange?

No. The contract must be between the intermediary and the builder. Inspections and approvals cannot be done by the exchanger.

Can the Exchanger control the proceeds?

No. Any money spent must be spent by the intermediary through a builders control account. Invoices must name the intermediary and all vouchers must be approved as to the form of payment.

Does the Exchange become invalid if construction is not completed before the end of the 180-day Exchange period?

The replacement property held by the intermediary must be deeded to the exchanger, before the end of the 180-day time period. Completion of the improvements are ideal but not mandatory. The value must be determined by the cost of the land including the finished improvements or by a valid appraisal to determine the value.

If the property is not completed within the 180-day time period, can the Exchanger instruct the builder's control to advance remaining funds towards future supplies and labor?

No. Paying in advance does not help — nor does buying the materials and placing them on the property. The labor and materials must actually be turned into real estate to be valid.

HOW TO INITIATE A DELAYED EXCHANGE

Deferred Exchange Sequence:

1. The owner contracts to sell the relinquished property and wants to create an exchange but the replacement property isn't ready to close and may not have even been chosen.

2. The owner requests that the qualified intermediary prepare the exchange agreement and coordinate the close of escrow.

3. The intermediary participates in closing the sale of the relinquished property and receives proceeds from the sale. These funds are deposited in a bank account.

4. Within 45-days, the owner identifies the alternative replacement property(s).

5. The owner negotiates a purchase agreement for the replacement property(ies).

6. The owner through the intermediary and within 180-days buys the replacement property(ies), using the proceeds from the first sale, and property is deeded to the owner to complete the exchange.

HOW TO INITIATE A REVERSE EXCHANGE

STEP 1:   No matter which type of exchange transaction you are completing always instruct your real estate agent to include an "exchange cooperation clause" as an addendum to the purchase and sale agreement on both the relinquished property(ies) and the replacement property(ies) used in the Exchange.

STEP 2:   Contact your tax and/or legal advisor as early in the reverse exchange process as possible to consult with them to determine the advisability and feasibility of completing a reverse exchange. Your qualified intermediary will consult with your tax and/or legal advisor to determine whether the replacement property or the relinquished property will be used in the reverse exchange.

This determination will depend on such variables as the type of property in the exchange, the lender on the property to be purchased, environmental issues, tenant issues, construction plans, vesting and entity title issues, and numerous tax considerations. Reverse exchanges are significantly more expensive than simultaneous (delayed) exchanges because they are more complex and require additional time and effort by the qualified intermediary to set up and administer. In addition, since the qualified intermediary must hold title to either the relinquished or replacement property(ies), to complete the exchange, the qualified intermediary has a much greater risk and liability factor doing reverses exchanges than in doing simultaneous (delayed) exchanges.

STEP 3:   Prior to Network Exchange (NE), or some other entity designated by Network Exchange taking title in the reverse exchange to either the replacement or relinquished property you must have hazard and liability insurance coverage naming Network Exchange as an insured — or additional insurance for the amount of liability coverage specified by Network Exchange. In addition, prior to taking title to commercial, industrial or raw land Network Exchange must be provided with a copy of the Phase 1 Environmental Assessment Report or other similar type of environmental evaluation for review and approval.

STEP 4: If Network Exchange is taking title to the replacement property you must contact your lender whether it is a financial institution or the seller of the replacement property and instruct your lender that you will be completing a reverse exchange and that Network Exchange or some other entity designated by Network Exchange will be the borrower on the loan until such time as the replacement property is deeded to you. Your lender can require that you be a guarantor on the loan and that you offer other collateral (other than the relinquished property), if necessary to meet the lenders under-writing guidelines. Network Exchange will work closely with your lender to assist them in understanding the reverse exchange process.

HOW TO INITIATE A BUILD-TO-SUIT EXCHANGE

STEP 1: Select a qualified intermediary to assist you with the "build-to-suit" exchange, as early in the process as possible. Key points to consider when selecting a qualified intermediary are:

- The knowledge and experience of the staff

- The professional assistance provided to your real estate agent, CPA and attorney

- The security of the exchange funds held by the qualified intermediary, such as Network Exchange (NE), which is of especially critical importance

STEP 2: No matter which type of exchange transaction you are completing, always instruct your real estate agent to include an "exchange cooperation clause" as an addendum to the purchase and sale agreement on both the relinquished property(ies), and the replacement property(ies) used in the exchange.

STEP 3: Contact your tax and/or legal advisor as early in the "build-to-suit" exchange process as possible to consult with them to determine the advisability and feasibility of completing a "build-to-suit" exchange. "Build-to-suit" exchanges are significantly more expensive than simultaneous (delayed) exchanges because they are more complex and require additional time and effort by the qualified intermediary to set up and administer. In addition, since the qualified intermediary must hold title to the replacement property to complete the exchange the qualified intermediary has a much greater risk and liability factor than with simultaneous (delayed) exchanges.

STEP 4: Contact your qualified intermediary as soon as possible after entering into a purchase and sale agreement for the sale of the relinquished property and advise the qualified intermediary immediately of the timing and close of the transaction. Both your attorney and accountant must approve the transaction before Network Exchange will finalize the exchange documents.

Network Exchange will work closely with your tax and legal advisors through every step of the transaction. Network Exchange will draft the appropriate exchange agreement, assignment, construction management agreement, and exchange closing instructions for execution prior to the close of the property being acquired as replacement property. Network Exchange will also assign into the construction contract as the owner (and may require a third party inspector to determine the progress of the work), and the disbursement of funds from the exchange account.

In a delayed "build-to-suit" exchange the construction work must be completed prior the end of the 180-day exchange period. If you determine that the proposed construction work cannot be completed within the 180-days then the exchange must be structured as a reverse "build-to-suit" exchange. Also, in a "build-to-suit" exchange the replacement property must be identified to the qualified intermediary with a description of the underlying land and at the time of the identification a detailed description of the improvements to be completed by the end of the exchange.

REMEMBER—DO NOT CLOSE ESCROW ON THE RELINQUISHED PROPERTY WITHOUT ALL OF THE EXCHANGE DOCUMENTS IN PLACE!

STEP 5: Prior to Network Exchange or some other entity designated by Network Exchange taking title to the replacement property in the exchange you must have hazard and liability insurance coverage naming Network Exchange as an insured or additional insured for the amount of liability coverage specified by Network Exchange. In addition, prior to taking title to commercial, industrial or raw land, Network Exchange must be provided with a copy of the Phase 1 Environmental Assessment Report or a similar type of environmental evaluation for review and approval. Finally, each contractor or subcontractor that is to work on the construction project must be licensed, have appropriate insurance, and a bond satisfactory to Network Exchange.

STEP 6: You must contact your Lender whether it is a financial institution or the seller of the replacement property and instruct your lender that you will be completing a "build-to-suit" exchange and that Network Exchange or some other entity designated by Network Exchange will be the borrower on the loan until such time as the replacement property is deeded to you. Your lender can require that you be a guarantor on the loan and that you offer additional collateral, other than the relinquished property if necessary to meet the lender's under-writing guidelines. Network Exchange will work closely with your lender to help them understand the "build-to-suit" exchange process.

LIKE-KIND UNDER §1031

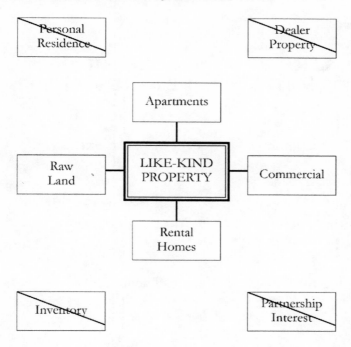

To qualify as "like-kind" any type of real property held for investment or productive use in a trade or business may be exchanged for any other type of real property to be held for investment or productive use in a trade or business.

UNLIKE-KIND UNDER §1031

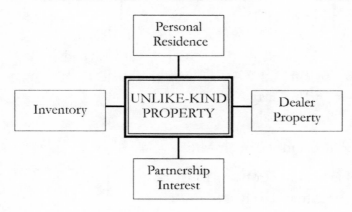

1031 EXCHANGE NON-SIMULTANEOUS (DELAYED) EXCHANGE

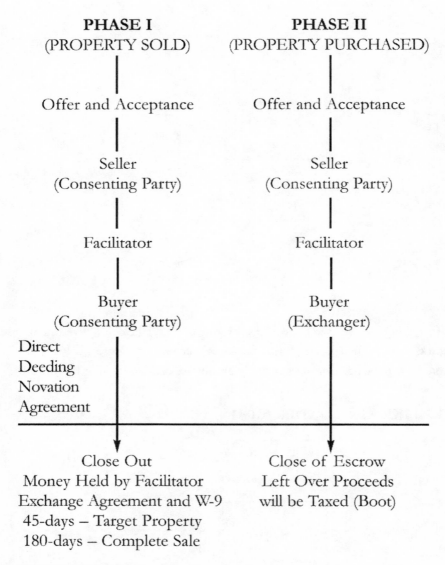

PHASE I
(PROPERTY SOLD)

Offer and Acceptance

Seller
(Consenting Party)

Facilitator

Buyer
(Consenting Party)

Direct
Deeding
Novation
Agreement

PHASE II
(PROPERTY PURCHASED)

Offer and Acceptance

Seller
(Consenting Party)

Facilitator

Buyer
(Exchanger)

Close Out
Money Held by Facilitator
Exchange Agreement and W-9
45-days – Target Property
180-days – Complete Sale

Close of Escrow
Left Over Proceeds
will be Taxed (Boot)

EXCHANGER Cannot Touch Money

Value of Replacement Property Must Be
Equal or Greater than Exchange Property

REVERSE EXCHANGE

Property (1): Intermediary holds replacement property until exchanger sells relinquished property.

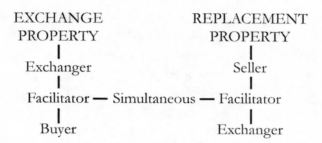

EXCHANGER must properly manage replacement property while intermediary is holding it.

Upon final sale of relinquished property to buyer proceeds will be disbursed to pay off debt of exchanger related to replacement property purchase.

PROPERTY (2): Intermediary holds relinquished property until a buyer is found. Exchanger takes title to replacement property. This method is used when exchanger needs to obtain a new loan to purchase replacement property.

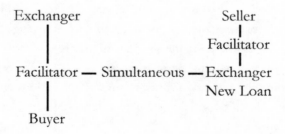

Excess funds from sale of relinquished property to buyer will go to pay off any loans or borrowed funds used by exchanger to purchase replacement property.

WHAT IS A "CONSTRUCTION EXCHANGE?"

The construction exchange, also referred to as an "improvement exchange," is a delayed or reverse exchange, in which the intermediary retains ownership of the replacement property and makes improvements to it. Once the improvements are made ownership is passed to the proper parties and the exchange is completed. The construction exchange provides property owners with more flexibility enabling them to either improve an existing property or actually construct a new replacement property.

TIME

```
                        ┌──────────────────┐
                        │   Exchanger A    │
                        └──────────────────┘
                                                    Property B
   Property A                  │        ▲        Plus Improvements
   $600,000                    ▼        │        $400,000 + $200,000

┌────────────────┐    ┌──────────────────┐    ┌────────────────┐
│    Seller A    │ ◄──│    Facilitator   │ ◄──│    Seller B    │
│                │ ──►│                  │ ──►│                │
└────────────────┘    └──────────────────┘    └────────────────┘
```

In performing construction exchanges a special trust account is often required for the intermediary to hold the proceeds from the sale of Property A. These proceeds will be used to make the improvements. The EXCHANGER determines which improvements are desired and makes arrangements for the construction. The invoices for the improvements are then forwarded to the intermediary. After obtaining permission to pay each invoice from the EXCHANGER, the intermediary disburses funds to the various contractors as the work is completed. A special agreement call an "ancillary agreement" describes this procedure.

The 180-day deadline also applies to construction exchanges. For the exchanger to have a completely tax-deferred exchange he/she must still meet the two basic requirements of; (1) having the same, or greater amount of debt on the replacement property, and (2) applying all of the proceeds from the relinquished property to the replacement property. After satisfying these two requirements the EXCHANGER can continue making improvements after the 180th-day. It is important to note that the actual improvements must be made to the replacement property. Even though funds for future improvements may have been released to a contractor within the 180-day period a contract to perform services in the future does not constitute "like-kind" property.

In the example, the EXCHANGER disposes of a property valued at $600,000 and wants a replacement property worth $400,000. There is $200,000 worth of taxable "Boot." The $600,000 cash from the sale of "Property A" is retained by the facilitator. $400,000 is used to purchase "Property B" up to $600,000. Once the work is completed the exchange is finalized and the property is passed to the EXCHANGER with a value of $600,000.

CHAPTER FOURTEEN

THE PROS AND CONS OF "CREATIVE REAL ESTATE"

Every "creative concept" is a vehicle to help buyers get more value out of their real estate investments. You have to be sure that the approach you choose is not risky even though it is "creative." There are lots of seminars given that promote "Nothing Down," "Foreclosed Properties," or "REOs" but you must be aware that most of these concepts have faults.

As the investor/buyer you need to understand that very few of the approaches that are advertised in the media actually work. When someone says that you can buy a property with "Nothing Down" you need to remember that they are not disclosing all of the facts.

When the real estate market is bad, seminars and direct-mail advertising pieces become more popular, and more people turn to "creative" approaches to sell their properties.

LET'S EXAMINE THE CONCEPTS THAT RELATE TO BEING CREATIVE"

Under the Equity Share Program the investor/buyer is looking for a way to get into the real estate market with the least resistance. Normally someone purchasing real estate as the investor/buyer needs a minimum of 25–35% down payment just to break even. Property management always creates a problem for investors.

My personal experience will give you some insight into the reality of investing in real estate. At the present time, I have over fifteen properties, ranging from single-family units, condos, 4-plexes, to 8-plexes. I can tell you that maintaining all of my properties could become a full-time job to manage, and maintain my investments. The loss factor, due to vacancies, repairs, and destruction became non-profitable over a period of time.

It is almost impossible to break even and if appreciation is low with no growth the investment will not work.

Most people make their money in real estate with a combination of factors:

- Always purchase at the right price
- Limit the amount of down payment money
- Minimize the monthly output (negative)
- Never purchase property with emotions
- Hold onto the property for at least five years

Always take advantage of the Tax Benefits

The concepts like "equity sharing" allow the investor/ buyer to do all of the above. Concepts like the "lease option" and the "contract of sale" allow buyers and sellers to get "creative" in a down real estate market. If you want to sell your property then what can you do to stand out from the other owners?

When the economy is bad most sellers are either losing their properties or discounting them to a point where a profit is unlikely. If you rent your property and your output exceeds the rental value, then you will be creating a negative cash-flow. Most property owners that purchased investments within the past few years are experiencing approximately a $1000 a month negative cash-flow. The other part of the puzzle is due to the lack of appreciation, the loss factor will compound and at some point you will be upside-down in the property.

The "creative" approach that might be possible is how to get rid of or maintain your properties with a minimum loss. If you are a seller and want to rent your property, consider a lease option the positive is that you will be guaranteed a monthly return of more than a rental value.

A lease option is basically a commitment from a renter/lessee who will pay more than normal rents to occupy your property with the possible right to eventually purchase the property. The renter/lessee feels that he/she is working towards purchasing the property at today's value. The extra time allows the renter/lessee to repair his/her credit, obtain enough down payment money, or sell an existing property.

The owner/seller is benefiting from the concept of a lease option, because, if he/she wants to just rent the property, it would generate a $1000 a month negative cash-flow. The owner/seller would need to sell the property and pay many costs, due to the current market conditions.

The lease option might work but if you do not monitor and work with the renter/lessee the reality is that only 30% of these types of transactions are able to be executed.

The renter/lessee, if he/she is able to make the payments and get credits towards the purchase has a chance to make the lease option work. I have done many lease options, and if you monitor the payments, get the benefits and improve the renter/lessee's credit a purchase might be possible.

Unfortunately, there are no tax advantages with the lease option. Always make the lease option for a long enough time to be able to adapt to the economy.

The "contract of sale" is also a viable source for "home ownership." Over thirty years ago I did many "contract of sale" transactions for many different types of properties. Initially vacant land contracts that wanted $500 down and $50 a month over a ten-year time period was a way to purchase property. The buyer got the benefits of ownership with terms, and eventually upon completion, they would obtain "fee title." Payments were monitored and protection of title was held by a third party.

Consider today where it's a buyer's market so that seller's are sitting on properties for over six months, and losing their investments. So many potential buyers have hurt their credit and even though they make a good income they are unable to purchase a property the conventional way. The average buyer makes $200,000 a year but if they rent then a good portion of their income is lost to taxes because there are no write-offs.

The contract of sale (equitable title) will allow the seller to get rid of his/her property and avoid the negative cash-flow. The buyer (vendee) can purchase the property at a good value with little down payment and eventually the vendor/seller will receive the remaining balance of his/her cash. The vendee will live in a house, have time to complete the contract, and get all of the tax benefits. The bad credit the vendee has will be repaired and they will hopefully achieve "home ownership."

If you are a seller and need to sell your property under today's market then consider a creative approach. The concept of protecting an investment is not only to prevent loss but to maintain a venue of how to solve a problem.

Do not get greedy when trying to either save an investment or steal a property. Remember the concept of short sales, REOs, and goreclosed properties do not guarantee a profit. In the chapters on short sales and foreclosures, I told you how to do the process, but remember I did not tell you how to invest in properties.

Purchasing properties using the "short sale" or "foreclosure" approach takes research and homework. The short sale process takes a minimum of three months, and eventually you might receive a value of $0.65 on the dollar for your investment. This sounds like a great advantage but remember it could only be good if all things are equal. If all parties cooperate then with time we might be able to purchase a property the bank is foreclosing on. Analyze the chapter on short sales carefully to get the procedures down. Remember, the concept of short sales is new and more approaches will become available to the consumer as time goes on.

I have been involved with foreclosures over the past twenty years and it becomes unrealistic to me about how people promote get rich by purchasing foreclosed properties. If you think that going to a trustee's sale at the court house is going to get you a property at a discount you are wrong. Seldom will you benefit from purchasing a foreclosed property at a trustee's sale.

If you do your research and are aware of values then you should be able to profit with foreclosed properties. First analyze the property, look at the value, get a property profile from the title company, and get comparative values.

Next contact an owner who is suffering a hardship and see if in some way you can help him/her with their situation. If you are a licensed agent then it is unethical to take advantage of a person under the duress of foreclosure.

You can always buy a deed of trust at a discount with the possibility of eventually owning the property. Discounts are usually 30% or more and as long as there is equity a profit can be made.

The reality of joint venturing is that this concept will allow you to benefit from your investment and will help the owner maintain his/her property. If the owner is willing to let you purchase the property then that creates it a winning situation for everyone involved.

To purchase depressed properties you must prepare well and always have an exit plan to your investment. Remember you can profit through "creative real estate" strategies but make sure you have a plan that will give you long-term profit.

This chapter is meant to help you understand the need to look at alternative approaches to real estate. Do the research, minimize the risk, and make good choices. You can be successful but analyze every investment and do not take unnecessary risks.

CHAPTER FIFTEEN

CONCLUSION

This book has been fun to write because it has taken me back to 1975 when I had to be "creative" to survive. Little did I know that, thirty-three years later, I would be going back to the drawing board to adapt to the current real estate market. The question you always want to ask is—What will the "Future of Real Estate" look like?

Throughout this book I have emphasized that the economy over the past twenty-five years has always fluctuated. There will be changes in the future – things like new laws, real estate tax rules and regulations and lending practices will dictate a new direction. One thing will remain constant is that no new real estate will be made. In other words the demand in the future will out-pace the supply.

In ten years your property values will double over today's prices. Investors buy real estate because it makes them money. Most of the wealth has been the result of investing in real estate. In California ONLY approximately 30% of the population can afford to own real estate. The growth in the Bay Area alone will increase in population by over two million people in the next seven years. The constant will always be "supply and demand."

Since the beginning of 2008, the following headlines have been addressed on the front page of the local and national papers.

January 6, 2008 – World Markets Tumble

January 16, 2008 – Median Home Prices Sink in Southern California

February 5, 2008 – Foreclosure Rate Jumps to 60%/Foreclosed Properties Sell Well

February 15, 2008 – Banks Eager to Wheel and Deal on Foreclosures

February 18, 2008 – Uphill Climb To Solve Housing Crisis (Bernanke Promises Rate Cuts)

March 12, 2008 – Stocks End Rough/Week On Down Note

March 16, 2008 – Bay Area Home Sales Slow to 1988 Levels

October 1, 2008 – Government Bail-outs

QUESTION: What do all the headlines mean to us?

ANSWER: A buyer's market exists. Sellers will become more creative to get rid of their properties, and the Federal Government will make changes over the next couple of years to adjust to the current market.

The other possible changes in the future might come true, but only time will tell:

- Capital Gains could be raised from 15% to over 25%
- Write-offs might change
- Loan guidelines will change
- More buyer assistant programs will be developed

MOST IMPORTANT OF ALL—"CREATIVE REAL ESTATE" WILL FINALLY BECOME MAINSTREAM.

In closing, I love real estate — if the objective is for the right reasons. I have been in the real estate market since 1975, and I have helped thousands of people achieve the "AMERICAN DREAM" of "HOME OWNERSHIP." However, in the end if we don't respect the value of doing investments the right way then it will not be worth all of the effort. Greed is not the right reason to invest in Real estate but security for the future is.

TERMS AND DEFINITIONS

Beneficiary – The lender on the deed of trust; the maker of the loan secured by the property and documented with a deed of trust.

Boot – Fair market value of non-qualified (not "like-kind") property received in an exchange. (examples: cash, notes, seller financing, furniture, supplies, reduction in debt obligations.) Receipt of "boot" will not disqualify an exchange, but the "boot" will be taxed to the exchanger to the extent of the recognized gain.

Conditional Sale – The sale of a property subject to certain conditions (e.g., lease house for one year with a conversion to ownership).

Constructive Receipt – A term referring to the control of proceeds by an exchanger, even though funds may not be directly in their possession.

Contract of Sale – A written agreement between seller and purchaser in which the purchaser agrees to buy certain real estate and the seller agrees to sell upon terms of the agreement. Same as "agreement of sale," and is also called "offer and acceptance" or "earnest money contract."

Conveyance – The transfer of the title of real estate from one person to another; the means or medium by which title of real estate is transferred (e.g., a warranty deed is most often used as a conveyance at the closing).

Deed/Grant Deed – Document that conveys fee title from owner/grantor to buyer/receiver/grantee. Must be legal and contain proper signatures and description of property.

Deed in Lieu of Foreclosure – A deed to real property accepted by a lender from a defaulting borrower to avoid the necessity of foreclosure proceedings by the lender. Does not wipe out junior liens.

Deed of Trust – A contract by which property is made secure for the payment of a debt, or obligation without a change of possession; a lien against the property, for money owed.

Deficiency Judgment – A judgment given when the security pledged for a loan does not satisfy the debt upon its default (judicial foreclosure).

Equity Build-Up – The difference between what you purchased a property for and what it's worth when you sell or have a new appraisal done.

Equity Share/Joint Ownership – Joint Investment between owner/occupant and owner/investor as a tenants-in-common interest

Exchange Period – The period in which the exchanger must acquire replacement property in the exchange. The exchange period starts on the date the exchanger transfers the first relinquished property and ends on the 180th-day thereafter or the due date (including extensions) of the exchanger's tax return for the year of the transfer of the relinquished property.

Exchanger – The property owner(s) seeking to defer capital gain tax by utilizing an IRC §1031 Exchange. (The Internal Revenue Code uses the term "taxpayer.")

Exercise Option – Written conditions under a contract that must be met at some future agreed upon time period.

Fair Market Value – A term generally used in property tax and condemnation legislation meaning the "market value" of a property (e.g., property taxes generally are assessed at some ratio of "fair market value").

Forbearance Agreement – Where lenders will let borrowers cease payments due to a job loss or emergency and make up past due payments at the end of the loan.

Some lenders will allow graduated payments, drop the interest rate, change the loan to an adjustable rate, or drop the mortgage insurance payments.

Identification Period – The period during which the exchanger must identify replacement property in the exchange. The identification period starts on the day the exchanger transfers the first relinquished property and ends at midnight on the 45ᵗʰ day, thereafter.

Joint Ownership – Ownership by two or more people (e.g., community property, joint tenancy and tenancy-in-common are all forms of joint ownership

Joint Tenancy – Ownership of real estate by two or more persons each of whom has an "interest" with the "right of survivorship." Typically used by related persons.

Judicial Foreclosure – Having a defaulted debtor's property sold where the court ratifies the price paid. (e.g., mortgage company is owed $50,000 on a first mortgage by the home owner). At "judicial foreclosure" the mortgage company bids $30,000 for the property more than anyone else bids. They then claim the property and are awarded a $20,000 "deficiency judgment" against the property owner.

Lease Option – (Rent-to-own) Conditional sale of real estate over a set period of time, with defined terms.

Lessee – Tenant of a property, who leases the property under certain terms and conditions (in writing).

Lessor – Owner of a property, who leases property to another party(ies) under certain terms and conditions.

"Like-Kind" Property – This term refers to the nature or character of the property not its grade or quality. Generally "real property" is "like-kind" as to all other "real property" as long as the exchanger's intent is too hold the property(ies) as investments for productive use in a trade or business.

Lis Pendens – A Latin term for "suit pending." Recorded notice of the filing of a suit (e.g., Notice of "*Lis Pendens*" is given to make others aware of the lawsuit pending).

Listing Broker/Agent – The licensed seal estate broker/agent who secures a listing of property.

Loan Ratio – Loan to value (LTV) in percentage to actual market/appraised value of property (e.g., $500,000 home with an 80% loan = $400,000 loan).

Memorandum – A condensed form of a document that dictates certain terms and conditions of an agreement.

Non-Judicial Foreclosure – Foreclosure on a deed of trust under the statues of the state.

Note – Obligation owed to owner of property. The terms of the debt are explained in the note that is usually secured by a deed of trust.

Notice of Default (NOD) – A publicly recorded notice that a property owner has missed scheduled loan payments for a loan secured by a property. The law requires lenders to record a notice of default to begin the foreclosure process. Starts the foreclosure.

Notice of Trustee's Sale (NOT, NT) – A document announcing the public sale of a property, to recover a debt owed by the owner of the property. The notice is mailed to all parties affected by the sale of the property, advertised in the local publications, and recorded in public records. Among other information it also provides the date, time, and location of the sale. Usually filed on the 90th day of the foreclosure.

Owner/Investor – Co-tenant who will not live in property, strictly treating ownership as an investment.

Ownership/Tenants-in-Common – (Fee title/ownership) actual ownership that will be divided into a percentage of value.

Payee – Lender on a note.

Payer – Borrower on a note.

Preliminary Title Report – Report issued by a title company before a transaction stating a willingness to insure title upon closing (e.g., the buyer arranged for a preliminary title report when the property was put under contract to discover whether there were any legal or title impediments to be cleared before closing.).

Purchase Agreement – A written agreement between seller and purchaser in which the purchaser agrees to buy certain real estate and the seller agrees to sell upon terms of the agreement. Same as "purchase contract, "agreement of sale." Sometimes called "offer and acceptance."

Qualified Intermediary – The entity that facilitates the exchange for the exchanger. Although the treasury regulations use the term "qualified intermediary," some companies use the term "facilitator" or "accommodator."

Quitclaim Deed – A deed that conveys only the grantor's rights or interest in real estate without stating the nature of the rights and with no warranties of ownership. Often used to remove a possible cloud on the title. A quitclaim deed is between a husband and wife.

Rate of Return – Return on investment; the profit over and above expenses that you receive on your investment (e.g., money, write-offs, appreciation).

Real Estate Market – The potential buyers and sellers of real property at the current time, and the current transaction activity for real property. It includes markets for various property types such as housing market, office market, condominium market and land market.

Real Estate Owned (REO) – Property acquired by a lender through foreclosure and held in inventory. Commonly referred to as "REO" (e.g., because there are a large number of recently mortgage Foreclosures, the bank's real estate owned properties).

Real Property – The rights to use teal estate. Sometimes also defined as teal estate (e.g., teal property includes but is not limited to:

- Personal residence owned in fee simple

- A life estate to a farm

- Rights to use land under a lease

- Easements and other partial interests)

Realtor® – A professional in real estate who subscribes to a strict code of ethics as a member of the local and state boards and of the National Association of Realtors®.

Re-conveyance – The document that shows satisfaction of a deed of trust; releases obligation. A re-conveyance must be recorded. The lender executes the document.

Relinquished Property – The property "sold" by the exchanger. This is also, sometimes referred to as the "exchange" property or the "down-leg" property.

Replacement Property – The property acquired by the exchanger. This is sometimes referred to as the "acquisition" property or the "up-leg" property.

Section 1031 Tax Exchange – Investor/owner, under a 1031 Tax Code Investment can take certain tax write-offs and deferrals (national) (e.g., properties must be exchanged or qualify for "delayed tax-free exchange," "like-kind property/real estate for real estate," property held in use for a trade or business as an investment). (Sometimes referred to as a "Starker" exchange).

Selling Broker/Agent – The licensed real estate broker/agent that brings forth the buyer.

Senior Lien – (First mortgage) A mortgage that has a higher priority as a lien over all other mortgages. In cases of foreclosure, the "first mortgage" will be satisfied before other mortgages.

Short Pay – A term used to describe a discount upon payoff.

Short Sale – A term used to describe a real property sale where the total sale proceeds are less than the total balance due against the property including the cost of the sale.

Subject to Loan – Taking over payments on a loan without formal assumption.

Tax Benefits/Write-offs – Under IRS Code owner/occupant and owner/investor can take certain tax benefits, etc.

Tenants-in-Common – An ownership of teal estate by two or more persons, each of whom has an "undivided interest" without the right of "survivorship." Upon the death of one of the owners the ownership share of the decedent is inherited by the party or parties designated in the decedent's will. Same as "tenancy-in-common" (e.g., a syndicate is formed using a "tenancy-in-common." Under this arrangement all of the investors have to sign the deed for the entire property to be conveyed. Each tenant may convey his/her share independently).

Terms – Conditions and arrangements specified in a "contract."

Third Party – One who is not directly involved in a transaction or contract, but may be affected by it (e.g., a trusted third party designated as escrow agent by the principals).

Title – Evidence that the owner of land is in lawful possession thereof; evidence of ownership.

Title Company – One in the business of examining title to real estate and/or issuing title insurance.

Title Insurance – An insurance policy that protects the holder from loss sustained by defects in title. Also referred to as "title guarantee."

Triple-Net Lease – Commercial and residential leases in which the tenant is to pay all operating expenses the landlord receives a net rent (e.g., pro-rated insurance, property taxes, mortgage, etc.).

Trust Deed – A conveyance of real estate to a third party to be held for the benefit of another. Commonly used in some states in place of mortgages that conditionally convey title to the lender. Same as a deed of trust.

Trustee – A neutral third party in a trust deed transaction. One who holds property in a trust for another to secure performance of the obligation. Has the power to foreclose or do a Re conveyance.

Trustee Sale Guarantee (TSG) – A more detailed preliminary report that includes anything affecting title of a property such as liens. Usually requested as part of a foreclosure process.

Trustee's Deed – Document conveying ownership of property to the highest bidder, at a trustee's sale. Same as a "deed of trust."

Trustee's Sale – A foreclosure sale conducted by a trustee under the stipulation of a deed of trust. The sale of the property at the specified sale date (e.g., when a deed of trust is exercised a specific trustee is designated. Upon default the trustee is authorized to foreclose the amount owed and put the property up for a trustee's sale. The proceeds of the sale are distributed by the trustee, according to the priorities listed in the deed of trust).

Trustor – One of three parties to a trust deed; the borrower or maker of a promissory note. One who creates a trust, and gives a deed of trust as collateral for a loan.

Vendee – A buyer on a contract of sale (e.g., the "vendee" is the party that pays for the real estate bought).

Vendor – Owner/seller on a contract of sale (e.g., the "vendor" receives the cash, notes and mortgage relief from the "vendee").

Vesting – The name by which the "buyer" holds title when he/she takes possession of a property.

FREE AUDIO BONUS
RADIO INTERVIEW
BY
KENNETH E. BEASLEY AND JASON LO GUIDICE
"HOW TO UNDERSTAND AND SURVICE IN TODAY'S REAL ESTATE MARKET"

This four hour interview will discuss different aspects of the current real estate market. This audio will allow the average homeowner and future homebuyer to understand the current economy. The learned knowledge will provide you with a better understanding on how to hold on to your current property or if needed what to do to get rid of the property with the least negativity.

The new purchaser must be aware of the new loan programs, the best values and the most secure approaches to investing in a home purchase.

Learn about alternative approaches to selling and buying real estate. The time is right to look at the best buyers market in years, and examine the creative approach to owning in today's market.

"FUTURE OF REAL ESTATE EXISTS TODAY"
The Real Estate Market Sucks, Now What?
Download Recording at <u>www.futureofrealestatecom</u>.
Value unlimited

BUY A SHARE OF THE FUTURE IN YOUR COMMUNITY

These certificates make great holiday, graduation and birthday gifts that can be personalized with the recipient's name. The cost of one S.H.A.R.E. or one square foot is $54.17. The personalized certificate is suitable for framing and will state the number of shares purchased and the amount of each share, as well as the recipient's name. The home that you participate in "building" will last for many years and will continue to grow in value.

Here is a sample SHARE certificate:

YES, I WOULD LIKE TO HELP!

*I support the work that Habitat for Humanity does and I want to be part of the excitement! As a donor, I will receive periodic updates on your construction activities but, more importantly, I know my gift will help a family in our community realize the dream of homeownership. **I would like to SHARE in your efforts against substandard housing in my community!** (Please print below)*

PLEASE SEND ME _____ SHARES at $54.17 EACH = $ $_____

In Honor Of: _____

Occasion: (Circle One)   HOLIDAY   BIRTHDAY   ANNIVERSARY

       OTHER: _____

Address of Recipient: _____

Gift From: _____ *Donor Address:* _____

Donor Email: _____

I AM ENCLOSING A CHECK FOR $ $_____ PAYABLE TO HABITAT FOR HUMANITY <u>OR</u> PLEASE CHARGE MY VISA OR MASTERCARD *(CIRCLE ONE)*

Card Number _____ Expiration Date: _____

Name as it appears on Credit Card _____ Charge Amount $ _____

Signature _____

Billing Address _____

Telephone # Day _____ Eve _____

PLEASE NOTE: Your contribution is tax-deductible to the fullest extent allowed by law.
Habitat for Humanity • P.O. Box 1443 • Newport News, VA 23601 • 757-596-5553
www.HelpHabitatforHumanity.org

LaVergne, TN USA
13 January 2010
169809LV00003B/7/P